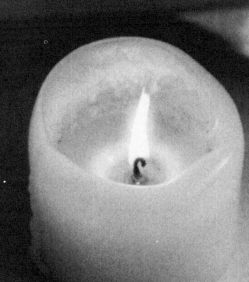

YOU ARE THE LIGHT OF THE WORLD.
A CITY ON A HILL CANNOT BE HIDDEN.

MATTHEW 5:14

city on a hill

Reflections on Our Spiritual Journeys

Compiled by Steve Hindalong

HARVEST HOUSE PUBLISHERS

EUGENE, OREGON 97402

CCM BOOKS

NASHVILLE, TENNESSEE 37205

CITY ON A HILL
Text copyright © 2000 by Steve Hindalong
Published by Harvest House Publishers
Eugene, Oregon 97402 and
CCM Books, a division of CCM Communications
Nashville, Tennessee 37205

Artwork Copyright © 2000 by Kim Thomas. The artwork in this book may not be reproduced without the permission of the artist.

Photography Copyright © 2000 by Dale Baker (in association with SPAnK!). The photographs in this book may not be reproduced without the permission of the photographer.

Scripture verses marked NIV are taken from the Holy Bible, New International Version®, Copyright © 1973, 1978, 1984 by the International Bible Society. Used by permission of Zondervan Publishing House.

Scripture verses marked NASB are taken from the New American Standard Bible © 1960, 1962, 1968, 1971, 1972, 1973, 1975, 1977 by the Lockman Foundation. Used by permission.

Scripture verses marked TLB are taken from The Living Bible, Copyright © 1971 owned by assignment by Illinois Bank N.A. (as trustee). Used by permission of Tyndale House Publishers, Inc., Wheaton, Illinois 60189. All rights reserved.

Scripture verses marked NKJV are taken from the New King James Version, Copyright © 1979, 1980, 1982 by Thomas Nelson, Inc., Publishers. Used by permission.

Scripture verses marked KJV are taken from the King James Version of the Bible.

Library of Congress Cataloging-in-Publication Data

City on a hill / Steve Hindalong, compiler.
        p. cm.—(A CCM book)
    ISBN 0-7369-0472-7
     1. Contemporary Christian Musicians—Biography. 2. Contemporary Christian musicians—Religious life. I. Hindalong, Steve.
    II. Series.
    ML385 .C55 2000
    782.25—dc21   00-033486

Printed in U.S.A.

00 01 02 03 04 05 06 07 08 09 / RDP / 10 9 8 7 6 5 4 3 2 1

A CCM Books/Harvest House Publishers Production

Art Direction & Design: Susan Browne, Susan Browne Design
Artist Photos & Black & White Photography: Dale Baker
Cover Artwork and Interior Paintings: Kim Thomas

Write us! CCM Books c/o CCM Creative Ventures, 104 Woodmont Boulevard, Nashville, TN 37205 or email ccmbooks@ccmcom.com
Visit author Steve Hindalong at the website www.thechoir.net

Thanks. . .

Windows of personal time are narrow and precious to each of the artists who contributed so graciously to this book.
Thank you all sincerely for finding the hours necessary to complete such essays.
I know it wasn't easy! Thanks also for your honesty—for risking self-exposure so that others
might be encouraged, and God our Savior glorified. In the light, we are free!

Thanks to my rhythm mate, Dale Baker, for hunting everybody down and shooting 'em (with a Pentax, that is).
The assignment required tenacity and finesse.

Kim Thomas, I'm so pleased to have been introduced to your art. Bless you for enlightening your world.

To Susan Browne, thank you for making everything look so good.

Congratulations to our editors, Terry Glaspey and Roberta Croteau,
whose task it was to guide a bunch of sailors (songwriters) into an orderly harbor (paragraph form).
Thanks for grabbing the chain and wrapping it around the post.
(Alas, another ambiguous analogy with which you must contend!)

To my friend, Robert Beeson, with whom I discussed for many months this "idea" that finally
became *City on a Hill*, an album and a book. Thanks with all my heart for the gig…
and for your interaction. Here's to the journey!

Eternal love to Nancy, Emily, and Erin.

It's good to be home.

city on a hill

Reflections on Our Spiritual Journeys

FOREWORD

After ten albums and seven hundred gigs (give or take a few) as the drummer and lyricist for a semi-renowned, marginally successful Christian rock band called The Choir—and having produced thirty or so albums for other groups of a similar description—I consider myself fortunate indeed to *still be at it.*

Spending much of one's precious twenties and thirties in recording studios and touring vans doesn't prepare a person for a whole lot else. And to be sure, such a lifestyle perpetuates adolescence. But you never know, someday you may need to know how to repack a trailer full of equipment to keep it from "fishtailing." And for someone who could never be called a "morning person," I've sure enjoyed the sweet chirping of birds at the end of many a hard day's night in the studio. No, it hasn't been a total loss. To the contrary. And anyway, I've gotta agree with Willie Nelson: "It sure is great to be makin' music with my friends."

That's what we did on the album we created upon which this book is based. And what a wonderful experience and challenge it was—coordinating the artistry and the ridiculous schedules of all the talented musical groups and individuals who participated. The artists were beautiful to interact with—divinely gifted and truly sincere of heart, each of them. And it was a soul-fulfilling privilege to offer these songs of praise and worship to the church and to the wind, as unto the Lord.

I admit to feeling a bit anxious when Roberta Croteau of CCM Books approached me with the idea of putting together a book to accompany the album. Sure, I had majored in English Literature, once upon a time in college—but I was the kind of student who showed up for class barefoot and fell asleep during Shakespeare. Since 1981 I'd written little else beside song lyrics. But I agreed to the challenge, provided I could solicit the participation of other artists and friends, some of them represented on the album, and others simply people I've come to admire as fellow believers, free thinkers, and creative souls.

But then came a second wave of apprehension. I wondered about my worthiness to accomplish such a goal and to speak to such a subject. Am I a "good

"Let everything that has breath praise the LORD."
(Psalm 150:6 NIV)

enough" Christian? Am I sufficiently "walking in the Light?" Truth is, if you knew me very well, you'd likely say "no." But God sees me as righteous because of what Jesus did. And He loves me even more than I love my own children—and that's a lot. So yes, I'll gladly take this opportunity to declare myself as one of His own!

In His Sermon on the Mount, Jesus told His followers, "You are the light of the world. A city on a hill cannot be hidden" (Matthew 5:14 NIV). As His disciples, we are what Dietrich Bonhoeffer refers to as "the visible community." Bonhoeffer asserts that Jesus did not say "BE the light." Instead, He said, "You ARE the light." It isn't for us to decide. We may choose, of course, to cover the light or hide it under a bushel. But what a privilege it is to let our light shine for the world to see—the blessed light of Jesus Christ in us! Not to reveal any radiance of our own, but to glorify our Father in heaven. To be seen kneeling at the foot of

our Savior's cross, on the mountain called Calvary, under the sweet light of His resurrection. A joyous honor, indeed!

I asked the individuals whose stories you'll read in this book to make the same offering—a testimony of faith in Christ. I asked them to be vulnerable, revealing their own flaws and sharing their own personal insights into their lives. I asked them to reflect on their journeys from darkness into light. I invited them to share their love for Jesus. That is what they have done. And each piece of writing is as unique as its writer's own spiritual path. My prayer is that you will find these stories inspirational, as I have. And I pray that all our hearts, words, and actions might bring praise to the God of wonders.

A City on a Hill cannot be hidden—let your own light shine!

Steve Hindalong

DALE BAKER

OF SIXPENCE NONE THE RICHER

Dale is a very musical drummer—creative and unselfish, surrendering always to the song. He's one of the splendid elements that make up Sixpence None the Richer. This City on a Hill project gave us an opportunity to make "the rhythm connection," and also to bond as friends. ❧ *He's an intriguing character—stylish (wears atypical wooly hats), yet humble. Whenever he exits a scene someone invariably makes a positive comment about him like "What a cool guy Dale is!" We all agree.* ❧ *And come to find out, he's quite the photography hobbyist—professional, no less. His handiwork is featured throughout this book. A Renaissance man!*

Pursuing God

*M*y view of salvation has definitely changed over the years. When I first accepted Christ as my Savior, I was not really aware of exactly what it was that I was publicly professing. For me, becoming a Christian was not so much a commitment as it was a rite of passage—just part of the deal of going to church. At a certain age you would go to a special class, learn to answer every question with a yes (or at least give a nod), and if all went well, you'd become a member of the church, be lavished with attention (which I desperately craved), and get a free Bible!

My junior high school experience consisted of being a "good kid" and a brief stint as a fervent disciple of Zig Ziglar's *See You at the Top*. "I'm supergreat, but I'm gonna get better" was my mantra, and Zig somehow convinced me that if I just thought positive things, I'd feel better. It never worked. Instead I just lost some of my inhibitions and became a good actor.

It wasn't until ninth grade that Christ really entered my life. It happened on the bus trip back from a Young Life ski trip. During talks and discussions on the trip, I had started thinking more seriously about Christ and what He had done on the cross and how I could respond to Him. I was convinced the Bible was true because I trusted the leaders of our youth group and from the Scriptures they quoted, it became apparent to me that I needed Christ. I talked it out with one of the youth leaders and prayed something to the effect of, "Lord, I know I'm a sinner, please forgive me. I ask You to come into my life and to change me into the person You desire me to be."

I really admired the youth leaders who led me and many others to Christ. They were excited about their faith, never seemed to have bad days, and were always smiling. They were also in great physical shape, having spent a lot of time working out. One of them even wrote a pamphlet comparing Christ's sufferings on the cross with weightlifting. As best as I can remember, the logic went something like this: If Christ was able to endure the suffering and pain at Calvary, then surely you can, as a Christian athlete, endure the suffering and pain of pushing yourself beyond your limits to win. Accompanying this thought was a drawing of a man struggling to bench-press a load of weight with the picture in his mind (illustrated by a bubble over his head) of Christ giving His all on the cross—struggling, yet bearing the weight of all of humanity's sins.

I saw in my youth leaders a model of Christianity that I assumed was the only way to be. They all seemed to have a deep relationship with the Lord, and I tried to emulate them as closely as I could. But for a shy kid with a poor self-image and no athletic skills or interest, this proved difficult. My efforts led me to confuse athleticism with piety. In years to come, as I inevitably backslid, my attempts to return to God were joined by equal attempts to get in shape, be physically fit, and become muscularly defined.

I understood salvation as little more than an insurance policy. The way I saw it, I could do just about anything I desired (with a few exceptions), and if I ever felt I was sinning or violating my conscience, as long as I asked His forgiveness, Jesus was obliged to pardon me. I held onto this kind of thinking throughout high school and most of college.

Toward the end of my college career, I was reading my Bible one day—all alone in my car—when I heard a loud noise. I immediately knew what it was. "It" was the trumpet of God. The trumpet of God had sounded, signaling the rapture of His saints to heaven, leaving all the sinners behind. I was in shock. I didn't see anyone else around. *Could it be? Was I left behind?* I couldn't bear the thought. I realized I had been making the mistake of believing that it really didn't matter how I lived my life. Instead, I'd seen salvation as a formula, that once the "magic prayer" of salvation had been spoken— "poof!"—one is immediately made impervious to damnation, no matter how damnable their actions might be. Although the trumpet turned out to be only the squealing brakes of a trash truck, I had been struck by the realization (revelation?) that I wasn't sure where I stood with God. This led me to examine my life and to begin looking for Him like I'd never done before.

I immediately went to the pastor of the church I attended, shared with him my experience (and another one involving a thunderstorm—but we won't go into that now), and pleaded for lessons. Most people would say I was "discipled" by my pastor, but I prefer to think he gave me lessons (not unlike the weekly music lessons I was receiving as a percussion student at the University of North Texas). I wanted to learn what it was I believed. I hungered for an education about God, the Bible, and living the life of a Christian. I'd never read the Bible seriously up to this point, and I now desired to know more about faith and salvation (was I truly saved?) and who Jesus really was. My pastor was very gracious, and if he thought me crazy, he never let on. He introduced me to some of the ways in which we can approach and read Scripture. He walked me chapter by chapter through the book of Matthew. For the first time in my life, I found reading the Bible to be exciting.

A few years later I met the minister of a scruffy little church near college who convinced me God *will* meet you in the Scriptures and that His Word is true. "You will seek Me and find Me, when you search for Me with all your heart" (Jeremiah 29:13 NKJV). I was also influenced by the lives and writings of Edith and Francis Schaeffer, authors of *L'Abri*, a book that had inspired my youth choir director from back home. And listening to the radio one night, I stumbled upon a program with Zig Ziglar, and he was challenging all his listeners to read through the Bible in a year. Zig was a part of my life once again and I rose to his challenge. In the year that followed the Bible came alive to me. It was exciting to see and experience God on a daily basis. Sometime later I joined a band called Sixpence None the Richer, and was introduced to the creative work of C.S. Lewis and other Christian thinkers.

I continue to pursue a deeper understanding of my faith. Recently, the professors and authors I've been introduced to by my wife (a seminary student) and members of the church we attend have been teaching me that our Christian faith is nothing without Christ, and that faith is more than "my" faith and "your" faith. It is collectively and communally "our" faith, and thus should be interpreted and worked out in the context of the community of believers, that is, the Church. I am so thankful for the people who have shaped and continue to shape my faith with their lives, conversations, and writings: G.K. Chesterton, Dorothy Sayers, Henri Nouwen, and countless others.

learning that my relationship with God is something that is continually growing and being touched by grace, not just a one-time decision.

So here I am. May the conversations and dialogue carry on. May we continue to encourage one another with the love, peace, grace, mercy, and patience that our heavenly Father shows to us. May we continue

A FEW YEARS LATER I MET THE MINISTER OF A
SCRUFFY LITTLE CHURCH NEAR COLLEGE WHO CONVINCED ME
GOD WILL MEET YOU IN THE SCRIPTURES AND THAT HIS WORD IS TRUE.
"YOU WILL SEEK ME AND FIND ME, WHEN YOU SEARCH FOR ME
WITH ALL YOUR HEART" (JEREMIAH 29:13 NKJV).

The people I find myself relating to on a daily basis are also being used of God to make me become more like Him.

In short, I'm learning that my pursuit of God has little to do with how much I can bench-press. I am

to live in right relationship with one another, not turning our backs when trouble or misunderstandings threaten. May we continue to strive for fellowship and communion. Most of all, may we continue to remember Christ our Redeemer—His work, His life, His death, His resurrection.

MARC BYRD

OF COMMON CHILDREN

A lover of beautiful sounds and sights, Marc is a man of extraordinary sensibility. He's a wonderful songwriter and a diligent worker—he shows no lack of intensity! ❦ *Having produced two albums for his band, Common Children, and subsequently involving him in several other musical endeavors, including* City on a Hill, *I've developed a profound respect and true affection for him. Ten years younger than me, I consider Marc my brother.*

Back Roads

I'll never forget how I felt about Michael when I first met him. He was a new student at the Christian school and he seemed plain to me—geeky, pale-faced, pig-nosed, his head shaved like a Marine. At first I didn't want anything to do with him. Instead, I hung around with the older crowd, and before the school year was over, I found myself, along with some other "troubled students," suspended for smoking marijuana. I was only twelve years old and was dealing with my parent's recent divorce the way so many kids do—I was desperately trying to become someone else.

I spent two more years at the Christian school and then decided to test the waters of public education for my freshman year of high school. It didn't last. The next year I was back in Christian school and, though it was a different school, in a small town like El Dorado, Arkansas, you carry your past with you wherever you go. Most of my old friends were there, as was Michael. But Michael was different. He resented the fact that his mother was the most disliked teacher at the school, and was on a mission to change his image. Out with the old and in with the new. I was happy to assist him with every step of his "makeover." It was the beginning of a relationship that would change my life forever.

Michael and I spent my first year at the new Christian school slowly getting to know one another. That was the year he got his old Dodge van. We laughed at it at first, but over time that van became our haven—and in times to come that van would haunt me in my dreams. By our junior year of high school Michael and I had really bonded with one another. Our connection began with music. He loved music, and I was the guitar player in a band that needed a rehearsal space. He offered us the use of his father's workshop out behind his parents' house. Soon every Saturday found us together. Michael would listen attentively and his mother would yell about the noise as we played with ear-splitting intensity. This was our weekly ritual for several months until we found our own band hall. Though we had to pay rent, we loved it. We were free from adults, volume restrictions, and rules. It provided us with a place of escape.

But at school, things weren't going well for us. By the end of our junior year, we had both been suspended— me for drinking and Michael for bringing gunpowder to school. I was planning on public school for my senior year and he'd be back to Christian school under the ever more watchful eye of his mother. But we still had the summer. In the evenings, after rehearsal, we'd take our chairs out onto the roof of the band hall and talk about everything in our lives. That Fourth of July we watched the citywide fireworks display from the comfort of our roof. The ice chest was never empty and there was plenty of pot to keep us talking for hours. And in our talking we found another place of connection—questioning religion and authority.

We had each witnessed our share of bad religion. My own experience of it started when I was nine. My parents, who were Episcopalians, went away for a weekend retreat. They came back different. I noticed a change in their behavior and asked them what had happened. They told me they had been born again and baptized in the Holy Spirit. But within a year of their experience they separated and then divorced. My dad eventually stopped going to church and my mom married the principal of my first Christian school. At the second Christian school Michael and I attended there was an algebra teacher who believed in what seemed like "conditional grace." One day we cornered her in the hall and presented a hypothetical situation. Here's what we wanted to know: If one of us was walking upstairs to algebra class and happened to stub his toe, reacted to the pain with a curse word, and then slipped and fell down the stairs and broke his neck and died, would he go to hell because he had not asked for forgiveness? Without hesitation she replied, "Yes, he would." We thought she was crazy. Then there was Michael's mom. She was extremely religious, but also extremely critical. Consequently, he was much closer to his father, who wasn't a very religious man.

By the time the summer before my senior year was almost over, I was no longer living at my mom's house. I wanted to graduate from a public high school and that nearly broke her heart, so I moved in with my dad. It was always a dilemma. If I went to Christian school, my mom was pleased and my dad was disappointed. If I went to public school, then my dad was pleased and my mom was disappointed. I couldn't win. The sad truth is that it was in Christian school that I first learned about drugs. So despite my mom's disappointment, and due to my belief that there was no difference between Christian and public school, I enrolled at El Dorado High School. I tried to get my act together before my senior year started, but it wasn't long before I fell apart again. The fact that Michael and I were now going to different schools only brought us closer together. I spent almost every weekend at his house. His parents had a motor home in their backyard that was usually well-stocked with food left over from his father's camping trips.

It didn't matter to us that the motor home was parked just outside the house. We felt like we were a million miles away from everything. We spent most weekends listening to music, laughing, and discussing existential philosophy. We drank. We got high. We helped each other get over bad girlfriend experiences. And we drove the back roads in his Dodge van. Michael always carried a small gasoline can in the back just in case we ran out of fuel. Some nights, when we drove out into the country, we would pull over and inhale gasoline fumes to increase our buzz. We were young idiots. When the night was over, we would drive back to his parents' house, crawl into the motor home, and crash. One Friday night, before leaving to go out, Michael and I decided to stock an ice chest full of beer and hide it in his father's workshop so that we could enjoy it later. When we got in that night, the ice chest was outside the shop door. We opened it and, to our horror, it was full of juice and soft drinks. There was a note taped to the top that read:

Enjoy the drinks. Talk in the morning.
Love, Dad

We were busted, but what a cool way to bust us.

The school year wore on and I became even more restless. I was searching. I abused harder drugs, like LSD and ecstasy, but the drug use only intensified my need to search. All the questions I asked in those late night conversations with Michael were beginning to consume me. One night I was staying over at the home of another friend. He lived about two miles from Michael. I got too high and felt uncomfortable. So I went outside and started walking. I walked all the way to Michael's house and found him in the workshop. I needed to talk. I asked him what were we going to do with ourselves. He didn't know how to answer, so he suggested the next best thing. He took me outside to his van and we inhaled gasoline fumes. I left Michael's and stumbled on through the back roads. I hadn't found the answer I was hoping for.

By this time, Michael had been kicked out of the Christian school and was on a special program that allowed him to earn his diploma at home and graduate early. Despite all of our stupid stunts, I had to admit that Michael could be pretty intelligent when he wanted to be. Thanks in part to his father, he could understand complicated manuals and engineering blueprints that no one his age could grasp. He would be getting his diploma before all of us and was thinking about his future. By now we had decided to go to the same college and to share a room. In addition to his studies, Michael planned to learn more about live sound engineering and would do sound for the band I'd form.

But despite all our plans for the future, I was still engaged in my own search for something more. Late one night I called my mom and rambled on like a desperate lunatic. I was questioning God, life, and the future. I hung up the phone and went outside. I crawled onto our trampoline and stared up at the stars.

The universe felt empty. So did I.

On March 1, 1988, I turned eighteen. My mom wrote me a special letter that I still have to this day. She had gone through many changes and we were becoming closer. In the letter she told me that the last year had been one of the most difficult ones of her life. She also told me that she had always prayed for me and, like most moms, believed that God had something special in store for me. My mother was no fool. She knew I wasn't doing well, but she still reminded me that there was Someone bigger than my sin and more true than all of my searching. On March 5, 1988, I had a horrible LSD experience. I unloaded everything on one of my friends. I went from one extreme to the other, first saying that I was God and in the next breath crying out that I had failed Him. I didn't sleep that night. The next morning I went to church. The preacher was a woman with a big black Afro. I was sitting in the back row with the rest of my friends when she raised her voice and said, "If He's truly risen, then what are you going to do with that truth?" Something happened inside of me at that moment. I left the church anxious, restless, and afraid. That night, I went home to my dad's house, walked into my bedroom, got down on my knees, and asked the risen Christ to save me. I meant it this time.

The next day, the world seemed less heavy, and I felt as though I was walking in a new light. I didn't have a vision of Jesus and there was no rushing wind. I just woke up with the peace that only comes from being forgiven. I wasn't ready to talk about it with Michael just yet, so I put it off until the following evening. I spoke with him on Tuesday night. It was a casual conversation at first, but then I told him that I was sick of drugs and tired of my life. It was time for a change. He agreed with me and invited me to hang out with him that night. He was going over to the home of another friend, Terry, to play video games. Normally I would have gone with him, but I had an important test the next day. We made arrangements to hook up on Friday. We'd use it as a time to talk about our lives and the future. We agreed to stay sober so that I could tell him my new secret.

The next day when I was walking to class, I passed by a close friend of Terry's. He asked me if I was going to see Terry in the hospital. I had no idea what he was

THE UNIVERSE FELT EMPTY.

SO DID I.

talking about. He told me that Terry was in ICU. He had been burned in a fire. "Did his house catch fire?" I asked in a panic. "No," he said, "it was a van. He was parked on a back road in the woods and the inside of the van caught fire. I think the guy who was with him is dead." I took off running and found my friend Jeff. I asked if he had heard what happened. He looked at me wide-eyed and said, "Terry's in the hospital—and Michael is dead. He burned to death."

I was chief pallbearer at the funeral. It was closed casket. Michael's dad could not stop weeping. He kept saying, "My son, my son, my beautiful boy. What am I going to do now? Oh God, what am I going to do now?" I had no answers for him because on the inside I was wondering the same thing. After Terry was moved from ICU, he told some of his friends what he remembered about the fire. They were parked in the woods. The gasoline can in the back had fallen over. They didn't notice some gas had leaked out. Michael held the can in his lap. He lit a cigarette and the van went up in flames. Terry was blown into the woods. He got up and tried to pull Michael out, but the fire was too hot. Terry burned most of the flesh off of his forearms trying to save Michael. There was nothing he could do.

I wish I could say that I don't miss him anymore, but I do. Sometimes it still hurts. I wish I could say that I haven't had any more experiences with bad religion, but of course I still have. As long as there is a faith that changes lives and hearts, there will be imposters. But more than anything, I wish I could tell you that my faith is always strong and that I always believe in God with the same certainty that I believe in Michael's death. Sometimes I doubt, and in my doubt I pray for faith. And through my faith, I find hope.

In his book, *Telling the Truth*, Frederick Buechner speaks of the difficult task the preacher faces in telling the truth every Sunday:

> The preacher must somehow present the silence and mystery of truth by speaking what he feels, not what he ought to say, by speaking forth not only the light and the hope of it but the darkness as well. *All of it*, because the Gospel has to do with *all of it*.

That is what I strive to do in my own life—speak and experience "all of it." And tell the truth about the light and the darkness.

Every Easter Sunday I think about Michael and the reality of his death, and I realize that when Jesus rose from the grave, He truly defeated the worst of all enemies. I am reminded every Easter that we have no resurrection without the cross, no life without suffering, no heaven without death, and no faith without doubt. This is what comes with living in a fallen world. So I wait for a new heaven and a new earth and in the in-between time, I walk on the back roads and I remember that no matter where I am, I'm not where I used to be. And I give thanks to my heavenly Father for His love and mercy.

PETER FURLER

OF NEWSBOYS

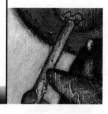

I felt something like a camel at an oasis a year ago, August, when I had the opportunity to hang out for a few days at White House Studios where Peter and his band, Newsboys, were recording LoveLibertyDisco. It was a season when my soul was weary. Peter and Phil (the longhaired mate) offered me refreshment—literally and spiritually—and we became friends. ❧ *Peter is adventurous—a risk taker—which is an element of his strong faith. He's willing to lead the way through the brush, swinging a machete. And he's following Jesus—who has made Peter a fisher of men.*

Seized By a Great Affection

I guess you would say I am a fan of music. Some of my earliest memories are as an eight-year-old living in South Australia when, unbeknownst to my father, I grasped for the family car keys, perched high on top of our kitchen counter. I would then proceed out the front door to the driveway, open the door of our late 60s FB Holden (Australian made), and slide across the blue and white metallic sparkle bench seat, being very careful not to touch the gear stick, the parking brake, or any foot levers along the way.

Next was my attempt at my first-ever big leap of faith— putting the keys in the ignition and being very careful to turn the key just halfway, so that the motor wouldn't turn over (and put me in the *Guinness Book of Records* as the first eight-year-old Australian kid to die of a heart attack). With the key in this position I could listen to the radio.

I had finally discovered the good life, the hot Aussie afternoon sun warming my face as I searched the AM radio airwaves for my favorite station. I don't remember the first time music caught my ears, eventually leading me to the family car radio. Maybe my love for music came from growing up with older sisters, whose music blasted from the duty-free Walkmans my parents picked up for them on their most recent missions trip. (I too was awarded one of these after the first car battery went dead!)

Twenty-five years later, I am no scholar of music—it would be a strain for me to tell you the difference between a Hungarian Minor and an EMG pickup. Or, if asked to comment on "the classics," I would probably start with Brian Wilson's *Pet Sounds* and end up at Bowie's *Space Oddity*, or perhaps something from that other great Brian—Eno.

This love affair did not start as a quest for knowledge about music—its beginnings, major composers, instruments, or even its present state. Rather, it started with how music affected me, where it took me, how

it made me feel. It's been quite a road from those sunny afternoons in the front seat of the Holden to my first tour with the Newsboys (1989) in our non-airconditioned, un-heated, un-reliable, and altogether un-conventional Dodge van.

I remember sleeping in that van, sweating until I stuck to the vinyl seat, traveling across Death Valley, California in the height of summer. I remember freezing in that van, wiping the ice off the inside of the windows during a cold New York winter. During this period there was always the music, unexplainably affecting me just as if I were still eight years old. Whether it was performing live each night with unbridled passion, until my fingers bled just a little bit, or sitting with my Walkman, wearing out the second cassette of Midnight Oil's *Blue Sky Mining*, the music had its impact upon me. It would kill time, soften the feelings of homesickness, or banish my frustrations about the heat and cold.

I didn't know the names of all the band members of Midnight Oil, nor did I know the chords/time signatures/names of songs—or even what some of the lyrics on that record were about. I didn't need to know anything about music for it to lighten my burdens, stir my emotions, or raise my thoughts to a better time or a better place.

My earliest memories of my faith in God have some similarities to my love of music. I never understood the Trinity, the Bible, Christians, Church, Baptism, Repentance, Faith, Reason, Conscience, Worship, or even grasped the fact that Matthew, Mark, Luke, and John were the authors of their respective books—I just thought they were disciples. I guess I preferred *to believe* than *to know*. I believed that God created the Heavens and the Earth and that He sent His Son because of our fallenness. Even though I did not understand how or why—I still believed this to be true.

Gradually however, this simple but beautiful view of the world—which many are blessed to carry from the cradle to the grave—grew dim for me in my teenage years. I found myself beginning to question the origins of this faith. Did I just believe because I was the son of preachers? Or was it because of countless Sunday school lessons, prayer meetings, and Bible studies? Had I been brainwashed? And these moral standards that I felt pressing in on me daily, did they come from a great Divine Intelligence, or just from my parents?

Because of all these questions, my next few years were filled with fear and confusion. One of my deepest fears was that I had been missing out on something, probably arising from hearing one too many over-glamorized, over-glorified church testimonies, many of which sounded a little more excited about how "lost" they had been than with how "found" they were now. I began to pursue as many manmade and earthly vices as I could find. Then there was the confusion caused by my conscience which, whether I knew where it came from or not, was still whipping me relentlessly, either rudely interrupting my daydreams or inviting itself into my thoughts in the early hours of the morning as I staggered home. Finally, there remained that grand old fear of eternal hell and its burning lake, which brought forth more pleas for forgiveness than there are sheep in New Zealand.

I finally came to the realization that I had no personal God, but instead the God of my parents. I realized as well that many elements of my conscience and my moral standard did indeed come from them. But I could not reject the truth that I saw portrayed in the daily lives of my parents or ignore the power I felt in their fervent, daily prayers for me. I saw them denying themselves what many their same age had accumulated or even what society said was needed, putting these things aside to carry the cross of Christ into all the world. I had to take a serious look for myself. I probably didn't realize it until a few years later, but at that time they were (and still are) that "city on a hill" for me, shining forth an example of the gospel, unknowingly challenging me to a search for a deeper understanding of this life and of things eternal.

So I sit here today in yet another bookstore/cafe in the middle of a very "taxing" tour (to say the least), and I can only attempt to do what (at this point in time) seems to be one of the most difficult things in the world for me to do—give an account of my faith, making sense of it with pen and paper. When we attempt this sort of thing, truly sorting through "that present wreckage" in our heads with the help of pen, paper, and maybe a little too much caffeine, it might be that it could get personal—a story filled with loneliness, insecurity, anxiety, lust, jealousy, temptation, failure, worry, and communication breakdowns with others, along with unexplained "glitches" in memory that can frequently overwhelm us to the point of losing the emotional battle.

However, in the last few years I have come to the realization that it became personal for God too—the great Author of life writing Himself into the pages of history through His Son, Jesus Christ. For 33 years Jesus walked the earth, experiencing what it means to suffer, to be lonely, to be tempted, rejected, abused (physically and verbally), and betrayed, even feeling the absence of God when His presence was needed most. "My God, My God, why hast thou forsaken me?" (Matthew 27:46 KJV).

In the words of Philip Yancey:

> Indeed, the suffering endured on Earth served as kind of a "learning experience for God." Such words sound faintly heretical, but I am merely following Hebrews: "Although He was a Son, He learned obedience from what He suffered elsewhere," that book tells us that the Author of our salvation was "made perfect" through suffering.

God took on human flesh and encountered evil and its effects in a different way than perfect deity had ever encountered it before. Then He brought forgiveness by taking on our sin. He defeated death by dying. He learned sympathy for human beings by becoming one. The author of Hebrews reports that Jesus became a sympathetic advocate for us. There is only one way to learn sympathy, which can be seen in the Greek root of the word that the writer of Hebrews used: *syn pathos*—to feel or to suffer with.

The book of Hebrews implies that because of the incarnation God hears our prayers in a new way, having lived among us and prayed among us as a vulnerable human being. In one of His last statements before dying, Jesus prayed, "Father, forgive them" (Luke 23:34 KJV). His prayer was on behalf of us all—the Roman soldiers, the religious leaders, the disciples who had fled in darkness, you, me—all of us who have denied Him in so many ways. "Forgive them, for they do not know what they are doing." Only by His experience of becoming a human being could the Son of God truly say with such understanding, "They do not know what they are doing." He had lived among us now…He understood.

I am seized by the power of this great affection—the Creator trying to win His creation back. I cannot be saved by any of my works or deeds. There is nothing I can do to make this Creator love me more, and there is nothing I can do to make Him love me less. I can only be made righteous through my belief—my faith—in this act of great affection. This doesn't mean that I have answers to all my questions. If I did, perhaps I would have no room left for faith. And I refuse to blame God for the bad things that happen in this life. Things didn't go that smoothly for Jesus while He walked the earth, either! Instead of constantly asking "why" things happen, maybe the wiser question would be, "What will I make of this?" As A.W. Tozer reminds us, "the living God is everything. Not success, not victory—but God. Not winning, not losing—but God."

Of course I still struggle with some of the same thorny issues about morality and conscience and the part God plays in it all, but as C. S. Lewis has so eloquently emphasized, everybody really knows there is a right and a wrong:

> I know that some people say the Idea of a Law of Nature or decent behavior known to all men is unsound, because different civilizations and different ages have had quite different moralities, but they haven't. They have had only "slightly" different moralities. Just think of what a "quite" different morality would mean. Think of a

I AM SEIZED BY THE POWER OF THIS GREAT AFFECTION—THE CREATOR TRYING
TO WIN HIS CREATION BACK. I CANNOT BE SAVED BY ANY OF MY WORKS OR
DEEDS. THERE IS NOTHING I CAN DO TO MAKE THIS CREATOR LOVE ME MORE,
AND THERE IS NOTHING I CAN DO TO MAKE HIM LOVE ME LESS.

country where people were admired for running away in battle, or where a man felt proud for double-crossing all the people who had been kindest to him. You might as well try to imagine a country where two and two made five.

It is certainly worthwhile to take the time to explore the intellectual basis for faith. I can personally recommend some authors who have been spiritual heroes of mine in this area: G.K. Chesterton, C.S. Lewis, Brennan Manning, Philip Yancey, Thomas Merton, Tolstoy, Dostoevsky, Kierkegaard, and A.W. Tozer. Writers like these help us to make sense of what we believe. But we must remember the limitations of a merely intellectual faith. All the evidence for Christianity can be just words until they are carried by the Holy Spirit from the book of apologetics into the human heart. Philip Yancey reminds us so well of what it is really all about:

I must admit that Jesus has revised in flesh many of my harsh and unpalatable notions about God. Why am I a Christian? I sometimes ask myself, and to be perfectly honest the reasons reduce to two:

1. The Lack of Good Alternatives.
2. Jesus.

Brilliant, untamed, tender, creative, slippery, irreducible, paradoxically humble. Jesus stands up to scrutiny. He's who I want my God to be.

CHRISTINE GLASS

Christy is, without a doubt, the best singer I've been blessed to record. Her heart is rich with melody. And she's a generous soul…self-sacrificial. Though she is as graceful as a feather, she will not be swayed by the wind. Her resolve is admirable. I care for Christy deeply. ❧ *By the time this book is published she'll be wedded to my close friend, Marc…so, she'll be known henceforth as Christine Glass-Byrd.*

Poverty and Light

Jeremiah was my grandfather. He's gone now, but I can still remember the musty scent of him, his patchy, wrinkled hand reaching out to hold mine. He was always an old man to me. I remember him as old and towering, bigger than anyone else—and when I had grown up a little, he became old and frail, as if his body might crumple and fall through the cracks of the floor at any moment. Eventually his mind kind of disappeared or maybe it just melted into something completely other than it was intended to be. So I never knew the real Jeremiah, the father of 12 children, three of whom died during his lifetime; the music lover who could play ragtime on the piano with such warmth and ease. I saw only the merest glimpses of that man, for by the time I was born he was fragile and hollow and lost in a dark sickness. In my young mind, there was no room for understanding darkness such as this. It was the kind of darkness that takes hold of light, twisting it around and around until you cannot tell the one from the other; a darkness that takes complete control.

Once, I found Grandpa's pills hidden under the dress of one of my dolls. He was convinced that my grandma was trying to poison him. It seemed possible to him that she just might replace his medicine with something sweet and deadly. In his mind, he was protecting himself from his sinister wife. All I could think was *"My grandmother? Trying to poison you? You mean the woman who waits on you hand and foot? The woman who has taken care of you for so long?"*

To be honest, I just didn't know how to respond to him. I can still vividly remember having to speak with him on the phone. I thought that if I pretended to be asleep, then my parents would let me off the hook. And sometimes that would work. I think they felt sorry for me when I listened to him ramble on the phone about religion. He told me more than once that the Baptist church would lead me straight to the steps of hell. He would preach on and on as I sat at the kitchen table with tears in my eyes.

As much as I tried to protect myself from caring deeply for him, when Grandpa finally died it was as though a flood poured forth from within me. My whole body convulsed with tears of profound pain and loss. Even so, it was still several years later before I could ask forgiveness for the selfish way I had treated him.

The greatest revelations of my life often come years *after* something important happens. The good news is that on my journey, I have found it's never too late to see the light. I have come to realize that any light— at any time—can help to navigate the way. I believe this with all my heart and all my experience.

I was so angry with my grandpa for so many years. Now I know that I was also afraid—afraid of becoming like him. That kind of fear doesn't go away with the mere passing of time. I understand that mental illness can be inherited from one generation to the next, just as we inherit so many other things. I am also beginning to understand that it's one of those mysteries I have no business worrying about.

I am a sensitive and an emotional woman. Just ask anyone who has ever worked on a record with me. I live my life and sing my songs with my heart always intimately involved. I think this was passed down to me from my mom. One of many gifts. My sense of

rhythm from my dad, my voice from my mom. A love of words from Mom and a need to figure things out for myself from Dad. And what did I receive from Grandpa? That's easy. I may not have known him well, but I know enough to say that he loved music—hearing it and playing it. Yes, this is our connection, and for it I am truly grateful.

I don't believe in reincarnation. I have no desire to come back and try this all over again as someone else. (I have a feeling I wouldn't do much better the second time around anyway.) I do, however, believe that just maybe God the Father is orchestrating my life in such a way that I am given chance after chance to get it right, in the hope that I'll eventually catch on. Since Grandpa died, there have been others close to me who have dealt with severe depression and worse. I like the fact that I have a few chances to use what I have learned. God is molding me, shaping me, and I can feel it.

I have lately become more acutely aware of my own spiritual poverty. Many hurtful things have conspired to strip away my self-consciousness and selfishness. My grandfather needed so many things that I could have given him—love, support, and understanding. As a young girl, I could not freely give those things to him because I was so afraid. Now, as a 30-year-old woman, I am still surprised by fear, but I have also been blessed with knowledge. I know that I am nothing without my Creator, my Father, my Savior. I have nothing I have not been given by Him. On my own I can do no good, and I have no light within that He has not placed there with loving hands.

And therein lies the truth that we all share, that draws us together. We are wounded, dying even, yet it is only in the broken places of our lives that His strength is uniquely revealed. He calls to us in our darkness and cares for us in our despair. And in addition to all this, He allows us to be part of the great love affair. He molds and shapes each one of us carefully—each body, mind, and soul—into His exquisite child. We are beloved and lovable because He is making us that way.

It is too late for me to help my grandpa, to reach out to him with the love of God. But it is not too late to see the light. It is not too late to walk with Christ and live in His presence with Him always before me. It is not too late to love and care for those around me. My Father has seen fit

AND THEREIN LIES THE TRUTH THAT WE ALL SHARE, THAT DRAWS US TOGETHER. WE ARE WOUNDED, DYING EVEN, YET IT IS ONLY IN THE BROKEN PLACES OF OUR LIVES THAT HIS STRENGTH IS UNIQUELY REVEALED. HE CALLS TO US IN OUR DARKNESS AND CARES FOR US IN OUR DESPAIR. AND IN ADDITION TO ALL THIS, HE ALLOWS US TO BE PART OF THE GREAT LOVE AFFAIR.

to drag me into the light. Sometimes I am haunted with images and voices from the past, memories that I cannot change. But on my clearer days, I have taken to seeing them as angels reminding me again to follow the One who made me.

I recently came across an old photograph of Grandpa and me. We are sitting at a table in the nursing home where he spent the last years of his life. I have one arm around him and a big smile on my face. We look happy, sitting there together. I didn't even remember that visit until I happened on that photo. It's coming back to me in pieces now and it's good and warm and filling me up with sentiment and longing. I think I'll take more pictures from now on.

Grandpa, forgive me for not spending more time with you and for not trying harder to understand you. Thank you for passing down your love of music through the generations and into my heart and soul. I have no idea what heaven will be like, but I guess that now you know. And I believe that someday we will be there together. Maybe we will sit at a piano and you will play ragtime and I will sing a perfect melody. And all of our loved ones will surround us, singing and playing their instruments to the glory of the One who made us.

I love you, Grandpa.

DAN HASELTINE

OF JARS OF CLAY

I've only recently become acquainted with Dan, but I recognize him as a man of conviction and God-breathed insight. He's a true poet—a leader and a compassionate helper. The Lord has beautiful designs for Dan far beyond the boundaries of his band, Jars of Clay. Of this I am convinced. ❧ *When you've finished reading Dan's essay, return immediately to the top, and read it again. Then, on another day, read it a third time. Listen for the voice of Holy God and be still.*

Hymn

Slowly, confidently, the train pulled away from its resting place. It had struck a deal with time and so rode away with the remaining seconds it would have taken me to climb aboard. The whistle sounded in triumph, betraying its joy over having caused another would-be passenger to slow down—if only for a few stolen minutes. I felt my heart fall like a coin tossed carelessly into a darkened well. I held my breath with anticipation of its reaching the bottom. I would have to wait. It was Chicago. Many trains would be setting out in the direction I needed to go.

COULD ANGELS DWELL IN THESE VERY ROOMS?
SURELY, THEIR WINGS COULD STRETCH TO THE EAST AND WEST
AND NEVER FEEL THE THREAT OF CAPTURE OR CLOSURE.
FOR ONLY GOD AND THE INFINITY OF HEART AND SOUL
COULD FEEL THE WALLS OF SUCH A PLACE
CLOSING IN AROUND THEM.
TO ALL SUCH, THIS WAS A HOME.

The train station was a cold mixture of marble and old wood. I surveyed the room. It was a drink wild with the intoxication of hurried commuters mid-pilgrimage, anxiously awaiting the first views of home. These were mixed with the defeated, abandoned scattering of those whose home had somehow eluded them or whose refuge this place of transit had become.

For the people with nowhere to go this was simply a time to dance along with the echoes of incoming and outgoing dreams. Their slumber took the shape of solace and became an escape from the reality, their search for home thus far was fruitless.

A different sort of sorrow erupted within me for the travelers who were only part way on their journey. And I saw others around me who had a clear destination, a lucid picture of the last few pages of this tragic and romantic journey. They were more out of sorts and bated in breath than their slumbering comrades.

Together we would wait. So lost in our travels, so insignificant within the scope of forever, so unwilling to notice.

My eyes wandered away from these various characters and toward the background on which the stage was set. I began to walk in rhythm to the predictable patterns of ancient gray and pearl-white squares. One missed square for every two tread under my feet, like a lethargic game of hopscotch. It took only a few moments to succumb to the trance-like awe that can only be felt in a place of such majesty. Is this a fitting home for a King, with its mile-high stone walls and a wealth of ornamental mastery? Not even a king could dare conquer the dreams or outsmart this court whose presence is made known in the rushing of the hour.

Could angels dwell in these very rooms? Surely, their wings could stretch to the east and west and never feel the threat of capture or closure. For only God and the infinity of heart and soul could feel the walls of such a place closing in around them. To all such things, this was a home.

So I took a deep breath and embraced the extremes that stood before me. The moment was like an old hymn billowing forth the immeasurable greatness of God and the all-too-measurable depravity of man. The clash of human mortality was on exhibit through leathery skin and charcoal hair. And the wild immortality which shone through carved granite statues under whose gaze Hercules would tremble and fall, had told a story of Gospel proportions. This is where David and Goliath crossed paths. And so I worshiped.

I heard the voice echo over the speaker, announcing that my train was ready to board. I took one last look at the "church" before me and stepped onto the train. I can only guess that the scheming of the hours to steal away moments of awe and wonder will never end. And the shortness of breath which renders our lips void of praise will forever cause our hearts to pound for things other than truth. So I am thankful for the hymns God blesses us with when we are forced to stop in our tracks and are inspired to worship.

RICK HEIL
OF SONICFLOOD

I hopped on board the SonicFlood tour bus for three days, intending to help with the production of their song for City on a Hill. That's right, they had a recording studio set up in the back of the bus! Technology failed us, however, and the equipment temporarily crashed. So we couldn't work to that end. But it was just as well. I enjoyed the ride, being a part of their world for a while, getting to know the guys a bit. Ah, the ol' road! Anyhow, that's when I met Rick, the bass guitar player. He spoke passionately of his love for Christ and his desire to serve Him. I found the conviction of his words and the fire in his eyes to be personally inspiring. The hand of God Almighty has touched Rick, and he knows it. I aspire to believing the way Rick does...to feel such burning passion for God.

Healed in Body and Soul

Miracles. I once heard someone ask a very provocative question: "Which is the greater miracle: For God to heal me? Or for Him to love a guy like me so much that He would sacrifice His Son?" In my life I've learned that it's not either/or.

I grew up in a church that believed the day of miracles has ceased. They taught that miracles stopped with the passing of the last apostle. Unfortunately, this theology left me in dire straits. You see, when I was in the sixth grade I was diagnosed with an incurable illness called Crohn's disease. Its symptoms include abdominal pain (caused by ulcers in the digestive tract), severe weight loss, diarrhea, emotional distress, blindness, heart problems, and, eventually, death. Because of this disease, I needed the personal touch of a God who still does miracles.

Besides the pain it brought into my life, my illness was a burden on my family. My dad operated a delivery truck and my mom taught preschool. Having a child who spent most of his time in the hospital was quite a financial strain for my parents. During my younger years I underwent two major operations in which a total of about eight feet of my intestines were removed. There were also long periods of time when I couldn't eat solid food and needed to be fed intravenously. The treatments I received, both in and out of the hospital, really took a toll on my family, and we found ourselves just scraping by. I felt terrible. I blamed myself for the family's financial distress and hated the fact that my disease was affecting everyone else. The pain of watching my mom and dad work hard but never get ahead because of my illness loomed over me to the point that I wanted to die. I thought I would always be defective—I thought I was doomed.

Though the physical and emotional pain of the illness never left me, as I grew up I somehow managed to cope by depending on prayer, my family, and music to get me through. Although music had always been a large part in my life, it was especially a blessing during those awkward, painful years. After school I would spend most of my time in my room, playing my guitar until dinner. Playing music gave me a purpose, and because it came very easily to me, it boosted my self-esteem. I was a member of several garage bands all through junior high and high school.

Then came college, and I knew it was time to get serious and start thinking about the future. I went to college for a year, then enrolled in a tech school to learn electronics repair. I repaired electronic musical equipment for about seven years, until one day, on my way to work, I realized there had to be more to being a child of God than just being a good example. I wanted to be *used* by the Lord somehow. So I prayed, *Lord, use me up! Whatever Your will may be, please lead me.* The next day I received a phone call from a guy named Randy, someone I knew from church. He asked if I wanted to try out for a Christian band called Big Tent Revival. I thought this must be an answer to my prayer—and it was! I played bass guitar with the group for about five years. During that time I grew spiritually and was blessed with CeCe, my wife.

Although I believed that God had placed me in Christian music, I found I wasn't quite up to all the traveling, and the symptoms of the disease continued to escalate until it was necessary for me to enter the hospital again. Unable to tolerate food orally, I was fed intravenously. CeCe stayed by my side throughout the whole ordeal, and she was the first person in my life to know that God was going to heal me (all that I am today I owe, under God, to my precious wife). She continually prayed in faith that I would be healed (Mark 11:24).

It wasn't long before the doctors decided I could finish my treatment at home. But once there my health took a downward spiral to the point where I nearly lost everything. The long, constant struggle with illness and pain had left me very self-centered. I had become a vacuum—always taking in, rarely giving; more concerned with my own needs than the needs of those around me. I built a thick wall around my heart in an attempt to deal with the emotional pain. The result was that I ended up empty, and any feeling of compassion was lost. I hated myself and began to resent anyone who loved me—including the Lord.

During all this I experienced something I never want to feel again. For the first time in my life I felt separated from Jesus. I felt a great heaviness that knocked the wind out of me. I became the prodigal son while still playing in a Christian band. I realized I couldn't live like this, and the mercy of the Lord did not allow me to dwell in this place of desolation for long. I finally yielded my life to the Refiner's fire and made the decision that, whatever should come to this earthly vessel—whether sick or healed—I would serve the Lord with all my strength. I was able to come to a place of humble surrender, then healing, and finally brokenness, because of His unconditional love and the continual prayers that were being lifted up to Him on my behalf (1 John 3:22-24). I became filled with a supernatural peace and convinced that *nothing* was going to hinder my relationship with God.

When I surrendered my life to Jesus, He removed Satan's foothold on my life and touched my heart and soul. I felt all the pain and turmoil I'd lived with for 22 years leave me. What a wonderful feeling— the indescribable feeling of a repaired body! Now it's as though fresh air passes through me instead of the pain and disorder I had known for so long. I'm

LASTLY, MY GOD TOLD ME TO PRAY FOR A BROKEN HEART,

A HEART OF FLESH RATHER THAN STONE. HE WANTED TO FIND IN ME

A HEART READY TO LIVE OUT THE GREAT COMMANDMENT:

"LOVE THE LORD YOUR GOD WITH ALL YOUR HEART AND WITH ALL YOUR SOUL

AND WITH ALL YOUR MIND AND WITH ALL YOUR STRENGTH."

THE SECOND COMMANDMENT IS THIS:

"LOVE YOUR NEIGHBOR AS YOU LOVE YOURSELF"

(MARK 12:30,31 NIV).

eating *real* food as opposed to being fed through a tube. Praise the Lord! Miracles still happen—Christ is the Healer! My Lord is the same yesterday, today, and forever! When my heavenly Father renewed my body, I fell at His feet begging for forgiveness and mercy. And without hesitation He lifted me up, threw His arms around me, kissed me, and renewed my soul.

Lastly, my God told me to pray for a broken heart, a heart of flesh rather than stone. He wanted to find in me a heart ready to live out the great commandment: "Love the Lord your God with all your heart and with all your soul and with all your mind and with all your strength." The second commandment is this: "Love your neighbor as you love yourself" (Mark 12:30,31NIV). There are no commandments more important than these. My heart had been broken by illness and by the powers of darkness to the point that it was numb and had lost all feeling. My heart was locked up inside an impenetrable fortress of self-defense, but the Creator of the universe was about to perform another life-changing miracle. Something that could have taken years of therapy, He did in a moment. God took that rock-hard heart of mine and allowed me for the first time to truly feel His love for me! That amazing love melted away the defensive walls that I had built. His compassion turned me inside out when the Good News finally got into my heart! A hot, passionate fire for Jesus started that day and I can say, without a doubt, that I'll never be the same! (Joel 2:12,13; Ezekiel 11:19,20).

In *The Anointing of His Spirit*, Smith Wigglesworth encourages me with these words:

> Therefore, with the audacity of faith we should throw ourselves into the omnipotence of God's divine plan, for God has said, "All things are possible to him that believeth" (Mark 9:23). It is possible for the power of God to be so manifest in your human life that you will never be as you were before; for you will be going ever forward, from victory to victory, for faith knows no defeat!

I am so thankful that our Lord died on the cross so that we may be completely restored—our minds, hearts, emotions, bodies, and, the greatest miracle of all, our souls!

STEVE HINDALONG

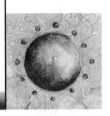

(Through the eyes of Terry Taylor) 🍃 *Down through the years I've greatly admired Steve Hindalong's formidable musical craftsmanship. He is one of those who has inspired me to continue to exercise my own humble gifts with passion and care by cultivating a work ethic that leaves little room for sloppiness or artificiality. He is one of the handful of Christian artists who continues to struggle for lyrical excellence, to find the most substantive and imaginative way to articulate their faith. Steve can be counted as one of the hardest working and certainly one of the brightest and best.* 🍃 *From the rich, imaginative word play that gave* **Chase the Kangaroo** *its bounce, to the heartbreaking— yet liberating—poetry of* **At the Foot of the Cross** *(arguably his and Derri Daugherty's most masterful work), Steve's exceptional gifts continue to be a wonder and an inspiration.* 🍃 *My friend Steve now brings his skills to writing prose and the reader may be confident he is in good hands...those of a true craftsman.*

Rhythm and Light

A sense of direction? I have none. I open closet doors trying to find my way out of friends' houses. I certainly wouldn't qualify to deliver pizza. And although I truly appreciate visual art, I never could draw—not a horse or even a cube. But I've always been in tune with the rhythm of life, with an instinct for keeping the beat. It was only natural that I became a drummer. I don't recall ever having to ponder the whereabouts of "the upbeat." (I'm referring to the "ands" of "one and two and three and four.")

The downbeat for me fell on November 29, 1959, my birth, my first glimpse of hazy light. So—I arrived just in time to experience the last 33 days of the decade that originated rock-n-roll. I was seven when Sonny and Cher sang, "The Beat Goes On," and 40 when Dick Clark exclaimed, "Happy New Millennium!"

In '66, I saw Jesus knocking—and heard Him too—so I answered. Here's my sentimental story, the details of which I've thus far neglected to tell. But as a large enough number of people have witnessed me banging ferociously upon a trap kit (drums, that is), well, I guess I feel secure enough to give an unabashed account now.

Hanging on my childhood bedroom wall was an artist's rendering of Christ knocking on a door—"the door to your heart," I was told. It was given to me by an evangelist who traveled with an easel, communicating the good news of salvation while drawing beautiful biblical scenes with pastel-colored chalk. My family attended not only Sunday night, as usual, but also the following five nights. "Revival Week," it must have been called. On Friday my dad and I won the "father and son look-alike contest," and that's why the picture was awarded to me.

Grace. I didn't do anything to look like my dad. And it was beyond my choosing to be born into a home with caring parents who exemplified Christian faith.

To never go hungry. To never be physically abused. To never feel unloved. Grace.

A few days later, I approached my mother and said, "I want to ask Jesus to come into my heart." We knelt together, and I did—and I believe He came in. Next, I insisted on being baptized—by immersion—the way I was accustomed to seeing the ceremony performed at Lindley Avenue Baptist Church in Tarzana, California. The pastor lifted me up into his arms so I wouldn't have to dog paddle and so the congregation of 50 or less could see me. I remember the pastor's wife singing, "Blessed assurance, Jesus is mine," nostrils blissfully flaring. And I knew the joy of such assurance.

But I was still unkind to my younger sister after that, broke a few windows, played with fire.

I've come to realize that God's plan to redeem mankind is simple enough to be understood and accepted by a small child. We are all sinners separated from God, who is holy. Jesus, His own precious Son, was born in the flesh, lived on this earth for 33 years, suffered and died—an innocent sacrifice. He was buried, then raised up on the third day, so that anyone who believes in Him might be saved and live forever in His kingdom. Yes! I believed this at six, and I'll believe it at 60. Still, I've barely begun to understand *who* Jesus is—this righteous One I am supposed to imitate. And what of the mystery of all mysteries, His infinite love? As Oswald Chambers has written:

> After the amazing delight and liberty of realizing what Jesus Christ *does*, comes the impenetrable darkness of realizing who He *is*.

I have a memory of a 1970 elementary school choral festival—and a dozen or so choirs performing as one. The song was "Hava Nagila," a Hebrew standard, and the tambourine part was not to be trifled with. It had to be played on the upbeats, and I got the gig because—well, in my humble recollection, I was the only one who could do it. Front and center, with no fear. (I even threw in occasional trills on the "ands" of "three.")

Now, after 30 years of shaking tambourines to the glory of God, I consider myself an authority on the subject to such an extent that I'd like to suggest a amplification of Exodus 15:20. Perhaps the Lord (and hopefully my editors!) will allow a paraphrase:

> Then Miriam, the prophetess, Aaron's sister, took a tambourine in her hand [and it was wooden and round with metal jingles. Woe unto any among you who craft or utilize half-moon-shaped, star-shaped, or most sacrilegious of all, fish-shaped tambourines; for such are heresy, and disagreeable to the ears of God and His saints], and all the women followed her, with [wooden] tambourines and dancing [and they hurled any misshapen plastic ones into a sea of fire].

Rhythmic enlightenment is a gift for which I offer thanks and praise to the Giver of all good gifts, my Father in heaven—and also to my father on earth, who drummed before me.

For my ninth birthday, my dad took me to a pawnshop and purchased a snare drum. I remember it like it was yesterday. He paid fifteen dollars for the drum, plus five more for the stand and sticks. Twenty dollars altogether. It was a lot of money for him at the time. Although his drumming days were done, he showed me how to hold the sticks and taught me the cadences from his high school marching band days. In fifth grade he gave me a cymbal. In sixth, a bass drum (with red-sparkle, waiting under the Christmas tree—and he'd touched up the black stripes on the scratched-up rims by hand) and a hi-hat. In seventh, a blue tom-tom. And in eighth, a white floor-tom. A red, white, and blue kit! I wish I still had it!

Thanks, Dad, for showing me true rhythm—for being the first one up in the morning to read your Bible…to pray…to make Mom coffee. Thanks for loving her—for celebrating servanthood. Thanks for keeping your old truck running because you knew someone would need to borrow it. Thanks for loving me—for embracing my individuality…my spirit…my music…for encouraging me season after season—and for teaching me how to hold the sticks.

Peace. The beat is divine—eternally true and absolute—as is light—as is love—as is God. Sometimes, when I'm in the studio shaking a shaker (a cylindrical container of mysterious earthy substance), I consider the presence of God's Holy Spirit in my life—how I so desire to be aligned with His perfect will—to trust and obey. I imagine myself chest deep in the Jordan River where my Savior was baptized. Carefully balanced, wet sand seeping between my toes, the steady motion of my outstretched wrist is even and parallel—as to the water line. And I visualize the white dove descending. Peace.

I met my wife, Nancy, at Azusa Pacific College. She was from Idaho and had never seen the California beach at night, so I somehow maneuvered us there on our first date. It was February 1, 1980. Under the moonlight, her eyes shone like diamonds. I was spun, smitten—gone. She was cute beyond belief and a beautiful soul—still is. For my twenty-first birthday she gave me a copy of *My Utmost for His Highest* by Oswald Chambers. She is a giver of good gifts. We were married in June of '82.

Around that same time I developed a musical partnership with Derri Daugherty that would eventually become The Choir. We recorded our first six (of ten) albums in six years, went through four bass guitar players, wore out five Econoline vans (for the glory of rock music and for the sake of the ministry), and discovered, but for the blood of Jesus, what wretches we truly are. I'll incriminate only myself.

NO, EVERYTHING WASN'T FIXED, AND IT STILL ISN'T. MY WICKEDNESS
STILL CAUSES SADNESS. MY BETRAYAL STILL LEADS TO DISTRUST.
MY TREACHERY STILL WOUNDS.
YESTERDAY I SINNED—AND I'LL SIN AGAIN TOMORROW.
THAT'S WHY JESUS WENT TO CALVARY, A CROWN OF THORNS PRESSED
UPON HIS SACRED HEAD—TO HEAL THE BROKENHEARTED AND SET THE PRISONER FREE.
I BELIEVE. AND I AM FORGIVEN—FORGIVEN—FORGIVEN.

I have always been appreciative of our Savior's first miracle—changing water into wine. I love wine—and vodka on the rocks (not too many rocks, thanks). Alcohol is a tremendous diffuser of reality's harsh glare. It's shelter in a glass; peace, joy, and love in a bottle. Spirits (not the holy sort) lure abusers like me into the erroneous freedom of darkness—but it is a darkness that enslaves.

So—lights on! I'm at a festival in Atlanta, under the influence—drunk, that is—and on stage—under the spotlight—making a mockery of any tempo. For an encore we played "Restore My Soul," which I was inclined to bring to a ridiculous climax, in typical rock-n-roll drummer style, with an onslaught of rapid, furious bashing, concluding with a leap into the air and the delivery of a final punctuating blow to the cymbals—the musical equivalent of "Thank you, good night!" Only this time I missed my drum throne on the way down and wound up flat on my back. It should have been an embarrassing moment, but at that point in my "career" I didn't so much care. And it was good for more than a few laughs. (There's something funny about a lot of sad things.) I had grown deaf to my Father's call—had fallen out of sync with His pulse—lost the beat.

There were other indiscretions. Cruel words slurred—forgive me, dear friends. Recklessness behind the wheel—God, have merciful eyes.

I tried to avoid the gaze of God in '89. It was just after the release of The Choir's fifth and most idealistic album, *Wide-Eyed Wonder*. That's when I wandered right down into the valley. Certain matters are best kept private, so I'll only say that I risked losing my truest treasure—my gift from heaven above. But Nancy held on to me tightly. We prayed together. We sought wise counsel. I opened my ears, my mind, my heart—and found freedom in the light. I turned my eyes once again toward the Lord of amazing grace, the Giver of peace, the Healer of my spirit. And yes, I found it to be true—He restores my soul!

No, everything wasn't fixed, and it still isn't. My wickedness still causes sadness. My betrayal still leads to distrust. My treachery still wounds. Yesterday I sinned—and I'll sin again tomorrow. That's why Jesus went to Calvary, a crown of thorns pressed upon His sacred head—to heal the brokenhearted and set the prisoner free. I believe. And I am forgiven—forgiven—forgiven.

Today, I built a garden. Well, it's not a garden *yet*, because nothing is growing in it. In fact, nothing has even been planted yet. That'll be Nancy's job. She'll forever be the tender of the garden. She drew a diagram for me to follow, so I tilled the soil, drove stakes, tied lines, graded the ground, mixed in peat moss and fertilizer, cut border timbers, and spiked them into the earth. And I remembered Jesus—His hands and His feet. Tomorrow I'll be a bit sore, but "ya know you're alive when you're feelin' a little pain" (I like to say that now and again. I'm not sure what it means, but I'm fairly certain it's profound). The sun will do its part, sure as our planet will spin in perfect time. Raindrops will drum gently upon tiny new leaves. Then, in the months to come, I will thoroughly appreciate whatever flowers, vegetables, and herbs my wife cultivates—and so will our girls, Erin, 10 and Emily, 12. I've so much to live for! Eternally!

Dear Father, thank You for blessing me so richly with family and friends. Thank You for creating me from dust, for breathing life into my soul. Thank You for sending Your Son to save me from death—for sending Your Spirit to lead me out of darkness. I praise You for Your sovereignty and for Your everlasting word. Teach me to see You even now, on this day—to hear You—to know You. Teach me to love others, thereby loving You. Teach me to dance in the fullness of Your radiant glory while celebrating the rhythm that is You in me, light from Light, true beat from True Beat.

TOM HOWARD

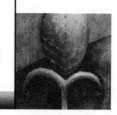

Tom is a man of devotion—to family, friends, God…and to his work. It seems as though the planet must spin a little slower for him than it does for the rest of us mortals, allowing him extra hours in a day. It's a mystery how he gets it all done—and so well! 🐚 As a composer and arranger he's amazing. As a friend…well, should I find myself in trouble, Tom will be among the first I'll call.

Listening to the Silence

I've always embraced the silence. I didn't always know this, mind you. I just knew that I didn't have a whole lot of trust for words or for the opinions of others. I didn't even trust my own opinions, for that matter. We receive a lot of information from the world, translating and categorizing it according to our own experience. We tend to allow our experience to become the standard by which we judge other people's actions and motives. But there is something deeper that speaks of the truth, a place in the center of God's silence where all of these considerations fly away like chaff in the wind. They become of no significance. In this place there is freedom and joy.

I had a fairly typical Midwestern church-kid upbringing. But as well-meaning as that culture can be, it was still characterized by a process in which we were spoon-fed all of life's answers before any of the questions had even really been formulated in our minds. We became a sort of "Mini-Me" to our folks, right down to our wardrobe, scrubbed clean and decked out in our little suits and ties. We took it for granted that our attitudes and patterns of behavior were God's way. And we believed that we were different from the worldly people we lived among. Because I grew up in the middle of it, I had no concept of how it created a contented isolationism that served to define what *we* were and what *they* weren't.

Then came a day that fractured some of my security about the simplicity of living. The delusions of my comfortable "business as usual" approach to life were undone by the Cuban missile crisis. Younger readers may not know of this event as anything more than a small paragraph in contemporary history books. But for me, as a young adolescent of 12 years old, it meant a period of time (72 hours, to be exact) when we were glued to our black-and-white Zenith TV and conversation around the dinner table dealt with the possibility of nuclear annihilation. The Russians had set up missile bases in Cuba, and there was a standoff between President Kennedy and Premier Khruschev that had the entire nation enthralled. The outcome of this conflict could, I understood, lead to the destruction of everything I knew and loved. And I realized I might die. It led me to look at life in a new way. Where do the seeds of such thinking plant themselves in a 12-year-old psyche? And how do they come to fruition? As the old Leonard Cohen song put it, "God was afoot."

In 1968 I was beginning my first year of college, and as all good Baptist kids did, I dutifully enrolled at Bethel College, my denomination's local citadel of higher learning. What I remember best was the confusion of Founder's Week, a week-long series of sermons and lectures aimed at inspiring the student population. Our attendance, of course, was mandatory. We sat through a "Who's Who" of Christian speakers that week. Each one got up and contradicted the one who came before. You had a rousing street preacher, who told us all to take our Bibles down to Fifth and Hennepin and get all the prostitutes saved. (There were a few guys that actually got dressed up exactly like the preacher, right down to the foot-long Icthus necklace. On the street you couldn't tell if they were there to save souls or save the whales.) The next speaker was a touchy-feely, sensitive type who admonished us to a gentle approach, telling us not to beat up on the downtrodden with our Bibles, but simply go to them and "hear their story and woo them into the Kingdom." Then there was the one who screamed at us for our spiritual laxity and called us all "the dead in Christ." Next, came a Zig Ziglar motivational-speaker type. And so on. The cumulative effect was one of utter chaos.

The Free Speech movement had been fomenting on the West Coast for about a year and the tumult was just taking hold in the Midwest. Our little college, generally immune to societal change, was starting to show cracks and fissures in its own foundational precepts.

One watershed event of that year (as this was during the Vietnam War) was the institution of the draft lottery. Each male was randomly assigned a draft number according to his birthdate. Any poor shmoe receiving a number lower than, say, 120 was likely to be immediately drafted into the army, trained at boot camp, sent to Vietnam, and summarily killed. That's how it felt, anyway. The day the lottery was announced there were two distinct factions on campus: really happy guys and guys who walked around with sweaty palms and a funny feeling in the pit of their stomach. I drew number 57.

I knew that, like any other upstanding middle-class patriot of the time, I had to stay in school to keep my student deferment; stay just as long as possible, too. After one year at Bethel, I transferred to the University of Minnesota and never looked back. My years at the University were marked by a systematic breakdown of what I thought to be my faith. What was actually going on, though, was that God, in His mercy, was stripping me of any vestige of religious pretense. My tendency to use my piety as some kind of social currency, buying acceptance and praise for my performance, had no comers in that godless environment. My faith "didn't work" anymore. I was in full drift mode and my rudder was somewhere far away, splintering against the rocks.

The years immediately following college graduation are a blur. I moved to California and drove a truck in Santa Cruz. The whole time I had my eye on Los Angeles. My career started taking shape when I made the move to L.A. and began to work with Larry Norman, a pioneer in early contemporary Christian music (we called it "Jesus rock" then). Our motley little crew worked out of Hollywood. The Solid Rock Records stable of artists was a colorful lot, made up of talented and somewhat disenfranchised souls. I fit right in. Randy Stonehill and Mark Heard were blazing their own trails. Steve Turner, a brilliant poet and journalist, would come by when he was visiting from

England. Other writers, actors, performance artists, dancers, etc., made for a continual parade of quirky characters in those days. Larry gave me my first real experience in the recording studio and taught me a lot about songwriting.

We had our personal differences, as all creative types do, but I always felt respected as a musician. We were that first wave of "real" musicians in the fledgling Christian market, our instruments our weapons in a cultural skirmish. (Does anyone remember when it was a sin to play a guitar in church?) We grew our hair long and stayed up till all hours. I traveled the world during that time, playing keyboards for Larry and Randy, and made numerous trips to Europe, Australia, and Asia. I was taking what tatters of faith remained after college and trying to express my beliefs with as much integrity as I could muster. Unfortunately, we formed our own "us vs. them" mentality, which led to our eventual undoing.

When we all disbanded, I moved into instrumental music and began writing for film and television, where I still find myself working much of the time. The old issue of, "Am I saying these particular words in a song because I believe them passionately or just to sell more records to a Christian demographic who wants to hear them?" simply dissipates when you make instrumental records. These records became my shelter. I was suddenly expressing my heart rather than propaganda.

I met my wife, Dori, in Los Angeles. I thought that we should get together about seven minutes after we met, but she took a little more time. We were married three years later. Within two years we had our daughter, Katie, and five years later Joseph came along. A question has been haunting me ever since the kids were born: How do I give them a foundation without imparting the damage believing out of duty did to me? How do I let faith be a marvelous process of discovery for them, rather than a chore performed to keep the old man happy? How do I do it right for them? Once again, the answer comes in silence and listening. Yes, I can give them information, but I can't make faith happen for them. I can convey knowledge, but I can't breathe life into their souls. That is the work of the Spirit. God says, trust Me. I love them more than you do. Get out of the way. Relax.

It is not only with my own children that I am learning to get out of the way. Sometime within the last two years, the prayer of "Thy will be done" graduated from the rote status it had held in my psyche to an impassioned prayer. I grew weary of hearing myself qualify my prayers, making them comforting and familiar. At some point, I realized I needed to take a stance of total abandon. When I did, the prayer came out exactly like this: "God, do what You desire. Do it to me, through me, at me, against me, for me, with me, without me. I'm Yours. Thy will be done."

On earth as in heaven. My soul waits in silence. Active, anticipating, rejoicing.

PHIL MADEIRA

Phil is among the more inspired musicians (and persons) I know—a truly creative soul. And he's not shy about expressing his opinions. Neither am I, so occasionally sparks fly. East meets west in Music City USA. But we are true friends for life. ❧ Joyfully, our two families go camping together. And Phil and I share membership in two churches—Saint Bartholomew's Episcopal, and also the one Phil calls "the every day."

The Church of the Every Day

*E*very weekday I rise, shower, and drive my daughters Kate and Maddy to school. It's a short drive, but one that I enjoy; it's my morning time with them. Along the way we listen to music; it could be anything—song demos of mine, an old Doc Watson record, or Terry Taylor's "Piehole" song, which has become one of their favorites.

When we reach the intersection of Tyne and Hillsboro, the music goes off, and we pray together. That's our "prayer spot." After we each make our few petitions and thanks, the CD player goes back on. Two seconds after we've said our "amens," it's a forgotten

moment, and I'm dropping them off at school. We leave each other with a traditional exchange: "The Lord be with you." "And also with you."

Though these simple things may seem nearly meaningless to the observer, I know that God has listened to our hearts and heard our brief prayers.

When I was growing up in the parsonage of a Baptist minister, the reality of Jesus was a normal part of every facet of our lives. I've often told friends that my parents' lives so exemplified what it means to live in God's presence that it was as if Jesus was lounging around on the living room couch. My mother says I accepted the Lord into my heart, as they say, at four years old. Such a youthful conversion carries its own set of problems. There is a real sense in which I, like many people raised in the faith from earliest memory, can lose my focus and forget that I've been saved from something. But along the way, I've become aware of my willful tendency to rebel and to make my own rules, finding creative ways to circumvent God.

I attended Taylor University in the '70s. There I experienced a form of corporate Christianity I'd never been exposed to before. Perhaps part of the strangeness of that time came from being in the flattest part of the Midwest, far from the Rhode Island beaches I had lived near for so many years and far from the healthy skepticism that New England is known for. This all combined to make me particularly sensitive to that which seemed left-handed or counterfeit.

I encountered a conformity to a regulated status quo that bothered me, an orderly little box which contained a neat and tidy concept of God and what it meant to be a good Christian. It felt as if God's cookie cutter had been set on automatic and had gone awry, producing several hundred bland sugar cookies. This is what I rebelled against. I didn't see myself as rebelling against the Lord, although in this period, I certainly extended the boundaries of grace, and most certainly sinned.

But in truth, God has no cookie cutter.

As the group of like-minded people I congregated with turned from faith, I was somehow able to keep my beliefs intact. Now, two decades later via the miracle of email, I'm hearing from some of these folks, many of whom have returned to faith, or perhaps are finding it for the first time.

Within the last three years, my wife, Elinor, and I have found our little church niche in a liturgical setting. Our parish does a wonderful job of combining contemporary and traditional worship. The prayer ministry among the members there is vital, and the church is small enough to keep track of the sick and the needy. It is a heartwarming thing for me to hear the name of my father (who suffers from Alzheimer's) read from a list of those who are sick. I feel a sense of community with my church because of this kind of caring.

I believe in Church. I believe that it's important to have some type of connection with other Christians, and that gathering together and lifting up Christ is a commandment. I also have come to love reading the prayers and the creeds together as a body of believers.

I like the fact that this group is confessing before each other our common belief in the essential elements of our faith. And I love taking communion with my family every Sunday.

My other church is The Church of the Every Day. It is made up of a ragtag group of people, most of whom are musicians or spouses of musicians. Some of us meet for coffee every day. Some of us gather at Sherlock Holmes, a local English pub and restaurant, every Wednesday night.

The beliefs that I confess on Sunday mornings take on poignancy during the week. In The Church of the Every Day, my friends and I subscribe to a similar set of beliefs. The opportunities to flesh out the message of the Gospels are many in everyday living.

When our friend Marlei was diagnosed with cancer, it was The Church of the Every Day that gathered around her, which is not to say that her own home church didn't. They were incredibly involved in supporting her and her family. But what a reassuring thing it has been to see our community of friends, all from different churches, joining together to encourage, help, and pray for a dear friend like this.

The Church of the Every Day is that group of Christians which sees each other on a frequent basis. It is the group that sees each other fleshing out the reality of what our creeds and prayers make claim to. It's the group in which one feels less pressure to be anything but one's own self, the group with which one feels the freedom to wrestle with doubt and faith. The Church of the Every Day is a sanctuary which many non-believers pass through, unknowingly, each day. From

They are often the friends who wouldn't even visit a "seeker church." Sometimes they are the waiters and waitresses in restaurants, like Pat and Moire at Sherlock's, the Wednesday night meeting place for The Church of the Every Day.

It seems to me that Christians often go about their daily lives trying to be different from the rest of the world. Well, it's one thing to try not to be "worldly," but it's quite another to avoid humanity. As we seek to

THE CHURCH OF THE EVERY DAY IS A SANCTUARY WHICH MANY NON-BELIEVERS PASS THROUGH, UNKNOWINGLY, EACH DAY. FROM ITS PULPIT, THE ONLY SERMONS DELIVERED ARE THE LIVES WE LIVE IN FRONT OF EACH OTHER.

its pulpit, the only sermons delivered are the lives we live in front of each other. I remember in the youth group of the church I grew up in singing "...they'll know we are Christians by our love." The Church of the Every Day is the place where each must put his money where his mouth is.

The skeptic, the unbeliever, and even the blasphemer linger on the edges, sometimes even finding themselves in the middle of The Church of the Every Day.

be like Jesus, should we not empathize with humanity? Should we not walk among the lost and seeking as He did, consoling the misguided, broken, and bruised travelers who were all created in His image?

The Church of the Every Day is the place where people who call themselves Christians worship every day. If, indeed, the Kingdom of God is a "city on a hill," then The Church of the Every Day is its front porch. May the lights be found on.

JULIE MILLER

Julie is admired by all who know her—for her music, and also for her character. Sure, she's just a bit eccentric (cares for fourteen cats, give or take a few), but she's also absolutely genuine. And although her manner may seem child-like, I feel like a child in her presence because of the depth of her spiritual life. Julie knows pain...and she realizes the love of Jesus. I've yet to encounter a more radiant person.

No Turning Back

I remember the dark.

I remember a time when I was not able to get onstage without chemical assistance. I remember walking offstage after concerts and wanting to hide in a crawl space or a trash can like a little child because I was going crazy from trying to pretend to be a tough, sexy barroom girl. I remember the odd comfort of saving pieces of broken glass, of hitting my head against brick walls, of taking entire bottles of things.

I remember looking at the faces of sleeping lovers and thinking, *You can't get close enough to me. I need someone in my head with me.* I remember feeling so incredibly alone, feeling like a stranger to myself, feeling like a child. I remember weeping into my pillow.

One night I heard a voice inside telling me it was time to end my life. The voice was not mean or threatening, just sort of calm and informative. At the club that night I noticed a broken beer bottle on the floor. I put the pieces in my pockets. A friend asked if I wanted a ride. "No," I said.

I don't remember cutting myself. Or screaming. Or much else my friend later told me I had done. I had disassociated myself, drifting off to someplace very far away. I do have vague memories of thinking, *Something's wrong, and when something's wrong you—go to the hospital!* "Take me to the hospital!" I told Larry, not understanding that the real problem wasn't just physical.

Another snippet I recall is the silhouette of a physician in a doorway. In terror I jumped off the examining table, taking the sheet with me, and crouched in a corner like a terrified child.

The next day, when my head was clear again, I found myself sitting in a chair in the hallway of a locked mental ward. After my failed attempt to escape with the janitor down the service elevator (those little foam rubber shoes and bandaged arms are a sure give-away), I raised a ruckus till I was given an audience with the head psychiatrist. He was the only one who could grant my release, so I did all I could to assure him I must get out or I really would go crazy. He asked me, "Julie, if you had three wishes today what would they be?" Time stopped. I looked down at my bandages and thought, *What do I really want? I'm pouring out my blood here for something, and I don't even know what the point is.*

Then I looked at the doctor and heard these words come out of my mouth, "I really have only one wish—I just want to know what the truth is. I don't know what it is. But I know there's something that just *is*. It's not relative—you know, *that* is true for you, but *this* is true for me. No, I know there's something that just *is*." Somehow, that answer satisfied him and he let me go. From that moment on strange things began to happen.

At that time, I wouldn't have said I thought Christianity was the answer. Having experienced the unique brand of religion that only the South can provide, I had concluded many years back that Christianity was some kind of club for people in the South, and the members tried to look alike, talk alike, and behave outwardly in a way that allowed them to think well of themselves. However, the very people who had hurt me most in my life had called themselves Christians. Growing up, I'd even called myself one. As a small child, I had asked Jesus to come be in my heart. But as a teenager, I was so depressed I gave up and went my own way. I lost myself in music, and when I got out of high school I joined a band. My self-value depended on how well I performed and how I looked—it was a tightrope from which I was continuously falling off.

I watched friends around me die, and the realization that I could die too terrified me. I went to bookstores looking for answers. I read about becoming one with the universe, as though we'd all finally get mixed back into the universal cookie dough of energy (this was supposed to be comforting?). Then one day, in the midst of my searching, my boyfriend Buddy moved the sofa. An old Bible was under it, taking the place of a missing leg. I began to read it.

I read about Mary Magdalene at Jesus' tomb. When she realized the gardener was actually her best friend, Jesus, come back to life, I felt elated with her. She must have been the happiest person who ever lived. I really liked that He would choose someone like Mary Magdalene as the first person to see Him again. Then I read on to where Jesus asked, "Peter, do you love me?" and I heard Jesus say to my heart, "Julie, do you love me?" The words were whispered with inexpressible longing.

About that time, Buddy came home with a new Emmylou Harris album. Suddenly I heard the most beautiful voice singing an old gospel song about how the straying sheep were sought by the Master, the One who gave His life for

"I REALLY HAVE ONLY ONE WISH—I JUST WANT TO KNOW WHAT THE TRUTH IS.

I DON'T KNOW WHAT IT IS. BUT I KNOW THERE'S SOMETHING THAT JUST IS.

IT'S NOT RELATIVE — YOU KNOW, THAT IS TRUE FOR YOU,

BUT THIS IS TRUE FOR ME. NO, I KNOW THERE'S SOMETHING THAT JUST IS."

them. I began to cry uncontrollably, touched by the tenderness of the shepherd, Jesus, who gave His life for us, His little sheep. I could feel Him searching for me.

Coming back from a show in Austin, I sat next to a Christian on the plane. He sent me a Bible. Later, I got on a bus in New York City (New York City!) and another Christian was sitting next to me. This was getting really weird. Around this same time, I came across a cassette given to me by a friend who was a Bob Dylan freak. I recalled hearing that it had some really fine Black Gospel singers on it, so I put it on. Indeed, Clydie King's backing vocals were as good as it gets. But what startled me was hearing Dylan sing "Gotta Serve Somebody" and calling us to choose between serving the devil and serving the Lord. Or when he asked the spiritually asleep, "When You Gonna Wake Up?" I listened and soaked up his message.

That night outside a club, I looked up at the sky. Pages of my life turned before me; pages of loneliness and hopelessness. And then, within my spirit, I heard these words, "I never meant for your life to be this way. I have always wanted us to be together."

Jesus—God—had always wanted to be with me? God had been lonesome for me? A foolish, selfish, self-obsessed pretender? This was too much. It hurt my heart. There was no condemnation in His voice, no scolding, no list of rules—just the deepest of longings. I began to weep, "I'm sorry, God. I'm so sorry." And as I wiped away the tears, I realized something inside had changed.

Everything else in my life began to feel really insignificant by comparison. What had once seemed so impressive looked phony, boring, and one-dimensional. I had a new and overwhelming hunger for the presence of Jesus (and I couldn't believe it). A few days later, riding with the band, I caught sight of a sign on a church as we pulled into the town where we were playing. It read: "Conference on the Holy

THIS WAS TOO MUCH. IT HURT MY HEART. THERE WAS NO CONDEMNATION IN HIS VOICE, NO SCOLDING, NO LIST OF RULES—JUST THE DEEPEST OF LONGINGS.

Spirit." While the guys went to the movies, I ran back to the sign. As I did, I felt invisible chains falling off me. There was a cross on the front of the church and I heard an inner voice saying, "If you keep your eyes on that cross, you can run the rest of the way."

Inside, the church appeared to be empty—so I read a hymnbook. I came across the old song, "I Have Decided to Follow Jesus." Suddenly, a man appeared and asked, "Are you Sister Ruth?"

"No. Nowhere close. I'm Julie."

I found myself explaining everything to him. The kind man asked me if I wanted to pray. We did. Then he said enthusiastically, "We're having a service on the Holy Spirit tonight. Why don't you come? And since you're a singer, why don't you sing a song?" The word "no" was on the tip of my tongue when, without having had any idea what I'd been looking at in the hymnbook, he asked, "Why don't you sing 'I Have Decided to Follow Jesus'?"

I knew it wasn't the man asking. And I couldn't say no to Jesus.

I asked to borrow their phone. "Buddy, you're not going to believe this, but I just gave my life to Jesus and I can't come back." Buddy was clueless, but he was also accustomed to my wide variety of odd behaviors, which probably prevented him from dying of shock.

Actually, I was the one in shock. *I'm in a church and I'm singing a gospel song to an entire building of Christians?* When the time came, I turned my back to the congregation and looked at the big cross in front of me. I hadn't remembered what the next verse to the song was, but suddenly everyone was singing:

The world behind me, the cross before me
The world behind me, the cross before me
The world behind me, the cross before me
No turning back, no turning back

And there was no turning back.

LEIGH NASH

OF SIXPENCE NONE THE RICHER

It was a stormy night and late when Leigh and Mark Nash, leaving Dark Horse Studios, encountered a "cold, wet, shivering little dog" (as Leigh described the sorry creature on my answering machine). She asked me to look for her sweater in the morning, since she had put it on "the poor, wet, sad, little guy"—not that she cared much about the sweater, it being "a ratty old thing, anyway." 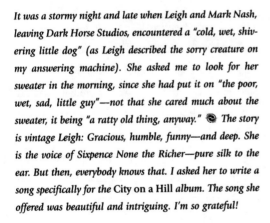 *The story is vintage Leigh: Gracious, humble, funny—and deep. She is the voice of Sixpence None the Richer—pure silk to the ear. But then, everybody knows that. I asked her to write a song specifically for the* City on a Hill *album. The song she offered was beautiful and intriguing. I'm so grateful!*

In Awe of Grace

I haven't always understood what grace means, but looking back over my life I can see how God's grace has always been with me. I did not grow up in a "model Christian home." As a little girl I went to Sunday school and "big church" every week with my mother and my sister. One of the things I remember most clearly is that my mom always seemed tense and moody on Sunday mornings. Perhaps it was the contrast she felt between her own life at home and the lives of all those happy, seemingly perfect families that shared the pews with us.

By comparison with their tidy little lives, ours was a life of tension and struggle and worry. When I was young, my father abused alcohol. And though he was never physically or verbally abusive, he left us all on edge most of the time because we never knew if he would come home sober or drunk. It was frightening and made all our lives feel out of control. But even then, in the midst of her own personal pain, my mother tried to keep me and my sister aware of God's reality and what He was doing in our lives. We learned valuable lessons about humility and forgiveness, that you could not truly love someone unless you were willing to forgive them. Mom taught us to keep our eyes open for the daily evidence of God's grace. She helped us understand that God was with us even in the hard times, His hand holding ours as we walked the rocky path that stretched before us.

Looking back on the years our family struggled so desperately, I see that God was working in us toward the eventual goal of drawing us closer together. He was using the events of our lives—the good and the bad, the painful as well as the joyous—to pattern each of us, through our circumstances, into a quilt of bright and beautiful colors. Only from the vantage point of today can I see the beauty and intricate pattern of that quilt. And be amazed by the grace that stitched it together so wondrously.

And God keeps stitching. It has to be God's grace that took a shy, nervous girl (me) and put her in the path of a shy, nervous boy (Matt Slocum) to create a band (Sixpence None the Richer). He gave us music as a gift and used it to heal our wounds so we could give back our music as a healing gift to others. Whatever success we have had is due to His grace. I marvel at what He has done.

I recently talked with a friend about my life today and expressed my grateful amazement at all the blessings that are mine: a wonderful husband, a successful singing career with people who continue to make it fun, and the healing that has brought my family so much closer together than I ever would have imagined. Not long ago, one of my friends said that all these things taken together are like God's warm hug at the end of a long, hard day. I can't help but agree with her. I am so much in awe of God's grace.

Trusting in His grace, I look forward to tomorrow. And I watch for the new patterns being stitched in my life even now by the Master Quilter.

CHARLIE PEACOCK

In 1986, when Charlie was producing Diamonds and Rain *for my band The Choir, he turned me on to chocolate-covered coffee beans.* 🐾 *Charlie has been a great influence on me. He's notorious for all his gifts and talents—as a solo artist, producer, author and spiritual leader—and for being a man of obvious integrity. Even after knowing him all these years, I still stammer when conversing with him. I admire him so.* 🐾 *But I've discovered that he is actually quite "down to earth." Only recently Charlie confessed to me that he had just finished reading an entire series of Louis L'Amour cowboy books. He asked me emphatically not to tell anyone, but...sorry Charlie, I made no such promise! Anyhow, the next day I picked up a cowboy book of my own.* 🐾 *Ride fast and shoot straight!*

The Bright Life

Something's wrong and I can't keep quiet. This world is so full of lousy thinking. My brain is filled with lousy thinking too. Since I'm part of what's wrong, I talk to myself about it. I rattle, skip, stutter, and try the best I can (with deft imprecision) to lock my mind around what might be called good thinking. Good thinking is, I believe, learning to think like God thinks. It is my fuel. It is the way of truth, the way of life, the way that leads me to God. Whenever and wherever I find good thinking I give thanks to the Good King.

I give thanks as I try to understand why a trout will rise from the river to take a certain kind of artificial fly. I give thanks as I attempt to comprehend the complex structure of a horse's hoof or what holds a hummingbird aloft. I give thanks to God for the 23rd Psalm, lovemaking, and my friend Phil Keaggy's mastery of the guitar. If it's got God-thoughts in or behind it, I'm thankful.

There is all manner of good thinking to be found in the Bible, but lots of really lousy thinking too. Like a great work of art, the principle of contrast is always at work in the Story—darkness and light. Since good travels in the brightness of light, that's how I purpose to travel as I make my way across the timescape of the hours I'm given. And while I'm traveling I write—drawing on the gift of words—trying to find ways that I can encourage and inspire others to love well through thinking well and doing good.

Years ago, while working in Leatherhead, England I came across an old sundial with these words engraved on it: "Count the Bright Hours Only." If you take Jesus literally, only the bright hours count. I think that's what Jesus must have meant when He said apart from Him we can do nothing. Of course I've done all kinds of things apart from Him. And

they were *something*. But I suppose the point He was making is that because those things were empty of Him, they are empty of any real worth or value. They carried no brightness, no light.

Jesus did nothing on His own, but only what the Father told Him. He was God-directed, about His Father's business. For little ones like you and me, the bright life is composed of doing what Jesus taught us to do. He's pointed us in a God-direction. Part of what makes life difficult is that we keep looking back.

Here is my prayer: I'm going somewhere new and I will not return to this place (call it the Dead Zone). I will not be the same again. I will be changed. After all, how can I follow the Teacher (the Light-Bearer), walk with Him, do as He taught, and not be changed? It's takeover time. Take me over, Teacher. I'm all Yours. I want to know what life is. If there's no life apart from You, then what is life in You? Teach me. This is my request.

How can any of us who profess to be followers of Jesus follow without knowing the answer to the question of what life in Christ is? Or what exactly the Father's business is? Perhaps our stories are the best evidence. When one sees a true follower, they really

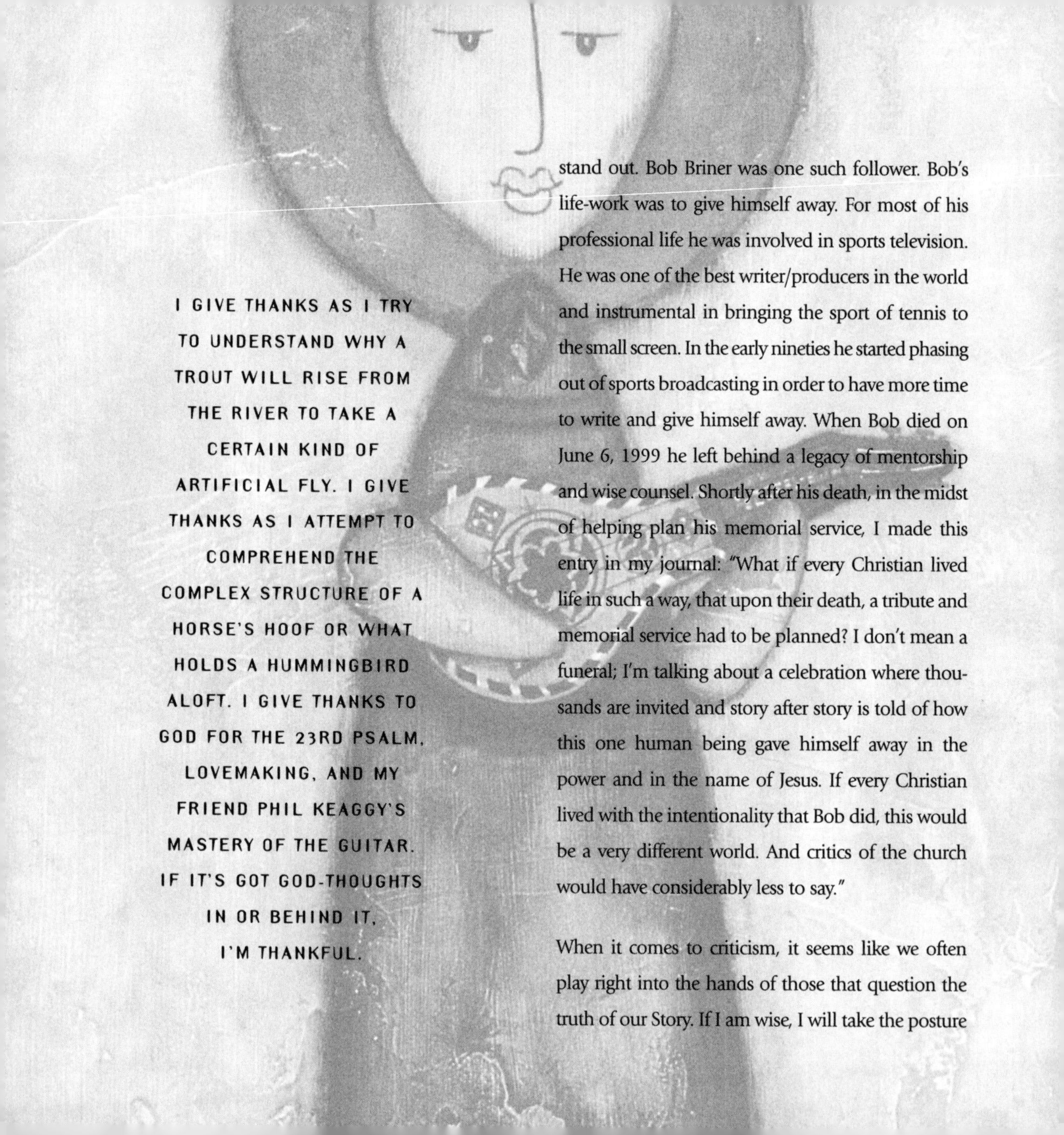

I GIVE THANKS AS I TRY
TO UNDERSTAND WHY A
TROUT WILL RISE FROM
THE RIVER TO TAKE A
CERTAIN KIND OF
ARTIFICIAL FLY. I GIVE
THANKS AS I ATTEMPT TO
COMPREHEND THE
COMPLEX STRUCTURE OF A
HORSE'S HOOF OR WHAT
HOLDS A HUMMINGBIRD
ALOFT. I GIVE THANKS TO
GOD FOR THE 23RD PSALM,
LOVEMAKING, AND MY
FRIEND PHIL KEAGGY'S
MASTERY OF THE GUITAR.
IF IT'S GOT GOD-THOUGHTS
IN OR BEHIND IT,
I'M THANKFUL.

stand out. Bob Briner was one such follower. Bob's life-work was to give himself away. For most of his professional life he was involved in sports television. He was one of the best writer/producers in the world and instrumental in bringing the sport of tennis to the small screen. In the early nineties he started phasing out of sports broadcasting in order to have more time to write and give himself away. When Bob died on June 6, 1999 he left behind a legacy of mentorship and wise counsel. Shortly after his death, in the midst of helping plan his memorial service, I made this entry in my journal: "What if every Christian lived life in such a way, that upon their death, a tribute and memorial service had to be planned? I don't mean a funeral; I'm talking about a celebration where thousands are invited and story after story is told of how this one human being gave himself away in the power and in the name of Jesus. If every Christian lived with the intentionality that Bob did, this would be a very different world. And critics of the church would have considerably less to say."

When it comes to criticism, it seems like we often play right into the hands of those that question the truth of our Story. If I am wise, I will take the posture of the teachable sinner and search the criticism for any good thinking, any clear insights, any evidence of truth. We have a tendency to mix the Christian message with our own set of political ideas and agendas or blur the line between faith and morality. We tend to be known more for what we hate and disagree with than what we love and affirm.

Our critics have a just basis for criticism if the fruit of our Christian discipleship looks a lot more like the lives of the Pharisees and Sadducees than those overtaken by the love of God, people such as the prostitute Mary, the taxman Matthew, and the murderer Paul. Or they can be justly skeptical when our version of the gospel life looks more like a life of materialism, greed, and self-absorption, seeking peace and safety at any cost, than a life of imitating and trusting Christ.

Which begs us to ask the question of whether we know what we believe? And what story our own life tells?

Here's what I've figured out for myself. My life is going to tell a story whether I intend it to or not. It's going to tell a story that says: This is what a follower of Jesus is, this is what they are about, this is what they believe, this is what they think is important. Because this is going to happen and can't be stopped, I better make sure I know my role and my job description: A Christian is a living explanation. As I go about living I will either make the teaching about God the Savior attractive or I won't. I make it attractive to others by living it out. Of course, it's attractive on its own, but my work should be to represent it accurately. That doesn't mean that my life is going to look just like His life looked. That's not even possible. No, I'll be doing well if I can become the kind of person He's teaching me to be. That's a big enough challenge right there.

I've decided my work is to tell the truth, to live a life framed and filled with God-thoughts about reality— what life really is. My goal is not to be a born-again Christian, a good Christian, a religious fanatic, a

IF THOSE WHO WOULD CRITIQUE MY LIFE CHOICES

DON'T SEE IN THOSE CHOICES THE DISTINCTIVE

TEACHINGS OF JESUS—WHAT HE IS FOR AND AGAINST—

THEY WILL NEVER NAME ME AS A FOLLOWER OF JESUS.

do-gooder, a spiritual person, a nice guy, or an American evangelical. No, I want to be an honest-to-God follower/student of Jesus, someone with a heart full of His brightness. Those of us who have been Christians for a while can veer from the path via the sickness of amnesia. Forgetting what we know (good thinking), we lose our minds and lose our way in life. With little or no connection to reality, our version of the Christian life becomes something that looks deservedly suspect to the world around us. There's often little distinction between our lives and the lives of those who do not profess to know Jesus. There's no contrast. No art.

If those who would critique my life choices don't see in those choices the distinctive teachings of Jesus—what He is for and against—they will never name me as a follower of Jesus. They will not mark me as a loving student of Jesus. They'll call me something else, and I don't want to be called anything else. I want people to ask: "What's the deal with him?" And I want the answer to be: "Him? Oh, he's with Jesus."

Here's another of my prayer requests: I want my life to look like it belongs to Jesus without having to announce at every turn that it does. It seems to me that a follower of Jesus can and should live in society as an active participant, yet in the process come to exhibit some distinctives that are characteristic of Jesus. I'm betting on this. If I start asking, "What is life all about?" I'm certain to find the answers from Jesus' teaching. Dallas Willard says that students of Jesus must trust that their Teacher has the best information on the most important subjects. I believe He does. They are called the words of life. Where else can we go to find such words?

What else can I do but "come and see"—and follow the brightness.

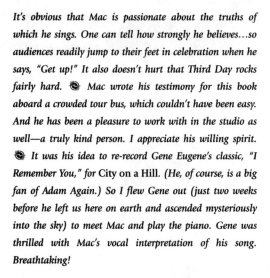

MAC POWELL

OF THIRD DAY

It's obvious that Mac is passionate about the truths of which he sings. One can tell how strongly he believes...so audiences readily jump to their feet in celebration when he says, "Get up!" It also doesn't hurt that Third Day rocks fairly hard. ❧ *Mac wrote his testimony for this book aboard a crowded tour bus, which couldn't have been easy. And he has been a pleasure to work with in the studio as well—a truly kind person. I appreciate his willing spirit.* ❧ *It was his idea to re-record Gene Eugene's classic, "I Remember You," for* City on a Hill. *(He, of course, is a big fan of Adam Again.) So I flew Gene out (just two weeks before he left us here on earth and ascended mysteriously into the sky) to meet Mac and play the piano. Gene was thrilled with Mac's vocal interpretation of his song. Breathtaking!*

Finding the "Blessed Assurance"

I guess my personal story of conversion is missing some of the classic elements. After all, I was never a difficult, troubled teen. I didn't struggle with drugs or alcohol or any other major addiction. That is not to say I've led a perfect life. Far from it. I have done my fair share of stupid things, things I should not have done. I still do. But I have been very fortunate in that I just haven't had to face many of the more difficult struggles that others have faced. And yet, there is always some drama involved in the story of any person's journey to faith. My story is no different in that respect.

I did much of my growing up in the small town of Clanton, Alabama. I lived there from the second grade through my freshman year in high school. Even today Clanton is a pretty small place, but when I was growing up it was even smaller. For a kid, about the only thing to do there was go to the skating rink or the high school football game on Friday nights. There was no movie theatre, no mall, not even a miniature golf course. On the weekends, the older guys in high school would drive around the town square in their "souped-up" cars and trucks. Round and round, over and over again. Doing nothing. I don't mean any disrespect toward Clanton when I say these things. I love my hometown and have many fond memories of growing up there, but it might help you realize just how small Clanton really was if I tell you that Russia had a McDonald's before Clanton did. Enough said.

I attended church with my family almost every Sunday. We were members of Providence Baptist Church #2. (I never did figure out where the #1 church was located.) It was a very small church with, if my memory serves me correctly, less than 150 members, a large portion of whom I was related to in some way. Seems like there were more bodies in the cemetery across the street than in the Sunday morning service. Mama always had a hard time getting my sister and me out of bed to make it to church on time, but somehow she managed to pull it off just about every weekend! I've grown to be grateful for her insistence on that.

It was in Providence Baptist Church #2 that I first started singing in front of people. Sure, I had been singing my whole life, probably since I could speak. But this was the first time I sang in front of persons other than my own family. My first solo was in a Christmas play. My part was just a few lines, but that led to the exciting opportunity of singing hymns on Sunday mornings in "big church." Now that may not sound like much, but to this little kid singing in front of a packed church of over 100 people on Sunday morning was like singing to a sold-out show at Carnegie Hall. I can remember how good it felt to make Mama proud every time I belted out a tune that was even older than the deacons in the front row. But though I sang those hymns with all my heart, most of the time I had no idea what I was singing about. My incomprehension was not only because the lyrics were filled with the old King James English —"thou," "thee," and words ending with "-eth" like "runneth" and "soweth"— but because the theology contained in these classic songs is sometimes hard to comprehend even for an adult, much less a little kid. Looking back on it now, I don't know whether the reason I never asked what the songs meant was because I was embarrassed to let anyone know that I didn't understand them or because I was just too dumb to know that I didn't. Either way, it led to a lot of confusion and questioning on my part. A lot of the adults thought I was the perfect little Christian kid because I could sing "Blessed Assurance." Unfortunately, there was no "Blessed Assurance" in my life.

One Sunday morning after having listened intently to the gospel truth for several Sundays in a row, I realized I needed Jesus. I may not have understood the doctrines of the Holy Trinity, predestination, or if I was a pre- or post-millennialist, but I could realize, even at 11 years old, that I was a sinner who fell short of God's glory. I knew that apart from the sacrifice of Jesus I was bound for hell. I understood that I needed to ask the Lord to forgive my sins and save me. And so I did.

I'd sat through many invitations given by the pastor before I worked up enough courage to walk forward and make a public profession of Christ and commit my life to following Him. I remember feeling God's tug on my heart that morning. The old wooden pew seemed even more uncomfortable than usual. I could feel the eyes of the preacher staring into my soul and I sank down in the pew and tried to hide from his gaze. I looked around and saw that no one else was responding to the invitation to get out of their seat and come forward. It would have been so much easier to follow a crowd of people to the front, but there wasn't even one person going. I finally stood to my feet and squeezed past my mama and my grandparents. I imagine they thought it was my usual trick of sneaking off to the bathroom. Instead I walked forward and accepted Christ. I think they were pretty surprised. And I was surprised when a flood of tears came to my eyes and I felt a burden lift from my shoulders. I prayed the "sinner's prayer" and was baptized the following week.

I'd like to be able to say that from that day forward my life brought glory to God in everything I did. But sadly, that isn't the case. A lot of the time my life was similar to those guys who drove around and around the town square in their "souped-up" vehicles, just doing nothing. I wasted so many years living my life for myself, forgetting the promise I made to God that I would commit my life to Him. But He was faithful in holding up His promises, even when I was not. Through all those years, God never let go of me. He never gave up on me. His mercy and grace were boundless. And they continue to be.

I've learned that there is no reason to play games with God, pretending everything is okay between you and Him. We can stop pretending and stop running from Him. He wants not only to save you and to give you a home in heaven, but also to give you an abundant life here on this earth. He has plans for you. Whether you've spent your life running from Him, or grew up in the church like I did, He invites you to have a relationship with Him. That is the blessed assurance of faith.

TERRY TAYLOR

A sentimental heart tempers Terry's wicked wit. His songs are hilarious…and brilliantly tender. So is he. He offers beautiful words. 🌹 *I've admired Terry since the late '70s when I used to attend Saturday night concerts at Calvary Chapel in Costa Mesa, California with my youth group. His band, Daniel Amos, was my favorite—and was the most controversial. They kept evolving, which seemed to bother some people—from cowboy hats to new wave, etc. But through all the phases they remained funny and great.* 🌹 *Anyhow, Derri (lead singer in The Choir) was once DA's "roadie," so our paths have intertwined. Some might say, in fact, that we followed our mentors down the road to commercial ruin. Nonetheless, we remain very proud of our association with those guys.* 🌹 *Terry is a dear friend, and still my hero. It's a relationship I treasure more than gold.*

Old Spice

 *T*here is a sweet, wholesome fragrance in our lives... we are a life-giving perfume" 2 Corinthians 2:15,16 (TLB).

I.

I caught the scent of Old Spice cologne today, and for me it is a memory echoing down the years and across the miles, bringing with it an unbearable yearning for someone lost to me, and the image of the child I once was....

Old Spice is my grandfather.

Grandpa wore it religiously, and he accumulated Old Spice collectible bottles over the years: the hunter's musket, the train engine, the Yankee Clipper. These specialty bottles gave me great pleasure as a child by fueling my imagination, their redolence and charming aesthetics often triggering in me little flights of fancy, of journeys across the sea or over the rails. I'm not quite sure what became of Grandpa's collection, but I'm reminded of it, and of the man himself, by an old western-style shirt that has been hanging in my closet since the day he died in 1982. The shirt still bears a slight trace of that cologne's unique scent, mixed with a good kind of body odor, earthy and rich with almost unbearable memories. One can especially catch traces of it around the collar.

A few years back, my wife and I were vacationing in Solvang when an elderly gentleman bearing an uncanny resemblance to my grandfather and wearing the same style of fedora hat Gramps had perpetually worn, happened to pass close by us on the tourist-crowded sidewalk. A slight breeze came up and delivered that familiar scent to my olfactories. Suddenly there was a lump in my throat and I was brought up short, unexpectedly overwhelmed with an exquisitely sad feeling of melancholy and a yearning for something unnameable. Grandpa's essence, his old spice, had managed to haunt me even there in the bright, bustling streets of Solvang.

II.

As a teenager I tacked a poster of the famous Michelangelo painting of the creation of Adam on my bedroom wall amid dozens of psychedelic rock posters. I had not been to the Sistine, nor was I particularly religious, but this poster somehow whispered something of mystery to me, something that resonated in the deepest core of my being, however indefinable, and so I placed it in a prominent place over my bed. Pictured on this poster is the Ancient of Days...His breath...His essence infusing His creation. God to Adam and Adam to God, finger to finger. Holiness touches what is now flesh and blood, offering this child of the dust the potential for glory or the freedom to slap that ancient hand away. By all appearances this was just another teenage flower child's poster hanging next to the "Fab Four" and the image of a young Mick Jagger. I could scarcely express at the time what hindsight, a little wisdom, and a few dark nights of the soul have enabled me to at least haltingly articulate today. "Keep in touch" read the copy on the poster, and I'm convinced that what I was hearing as a teenager, and would hear again from time to time down through the years (including some 31 years later on a sidewalk in Solvang), was an intimation of the Truth behind our best and most heartbreaking memories, the Holy Object of all our deepest desires and longings. "Keep in touch"...the whisper of God, the gentle nudge of Christ towards His glorious light.

Many of us can attest to getting these "holy nudges" from time to time, although we tend to label them something like "fond memories" or "melancholy." A friend of my wife tells the story of passing by a bakery one day when the scent of fresh baked bread invoked an image so pristine that she could hardly breathe. She said it was less memory than a "vision" in which she could see herself as a young girl in the kitchen with her grandmother, helping her to bake fresh bread. In a flash she could feel the texture of the bread, could see the bright yellow pat of real butter slowly melting on the fragrant warm slice, could remember the bread's exquisite mouth-watering taste. But what broke her heart, she said, was the radiant joy she saw on the child's face and that of her grandmother. Had bread ever tasted that good since? What had become of that young girl? And so it was there, next to the bakery on a seemingly ordinary day, filled with the hubbub of life that would shortly envelop her again, that she found herself slumped against a signpost, head in hand, and sobbing like a child.

If given the chance, most of us would take hold of what we perceive to be the best of what life has given us, would take a memory such as that of my wife's friend, and would wrap flesh and blood back around it and stay within its shining borders

forever. If heaven exists, we think, it would be—it must be—something like this, something akin to the smell of fresh baked bread and a contented child delicately brushing butter and crumbs from her lips as Grandmother reaches out and gently touches her under the chin. Perhaps the old woman had her own vision of heaven in that moment. Perhaps her dimmed old eyes shined bright again with the incandescence of another place and time long, long ago when she herself was a young girl helping Mama or Grandma bake bread in the kitchen. The aroma of bread from a bakery may indeed remind us of someone who is no longer in this world and, like the communion of Christ, by God's grace, transpose our recollection into a Holy Thing, a kind of sacrament by which we not only celebrate and honor that life, but perceive with spiritual eyes the Source of all life. We do this by prayerfully seeing beyond the memory to the one true Wellspring of all our deepest yearnings.

Our longing for home is more than likely a desire for Home Eternal. The soul may indeed sigh for a thing lost, but since we see through a glass darkly only the Spirit of God can fully know the true object of our deepest desire, and though these may come in the guise of Old Spice or fresh baked bread, they are nevertheless longings for God Himself. Countless visceral reminders surround us at every turn, sometimes in the form of an aromatic tap on the shoulder. They contain the potential to draw us closer to our citizenship in the "city on a hill," where we are called to be testaments to the glorious radiance of God's only Son. We often miss these little "nudges" because we have a deadline to meet, scheduled appointments, groceries yet to buy. Then, inexplicably in the course of the day, someone somewhere smells the scent of—let's say, cherry-scented pipe tobacco, and is suddenly reminded of Uncle Earl—("God rest his soul—hadn't thought of him in years"). Someone hears a distant train whistle and is reminded of Ol' Blue, long dead and gone, who would howl at the passing of each train. Someone hears a nostalgic tune being played on a distant radio, and although they've heard that same song dozens of times, for some reason this time they are flooded with a desire for something beyond their mental grasp, something strangely intangible, unnameable, and fleeting, like an object along the lines of our peripheral vision that is gone when we turn to face it head on. A teenager hangs a poster on his wall. An elderly gentleman wearing Old Spice passes a stranger on the street...something mysterious emerges from the commonplace, rich with the prospect of epiphany. To some the smell of Old Spice is nothing special, just the scent of a reasonably priced concoction of fragrance, alcohol, and water, available at supermarkets and fine drugstores everywhere. For another it may well be the whisper of God...

III.

And now I'm thinking of other savory smells, but heartier ones this time, like the kind that woke a young child from his sleep on a certain Saturday morning in the early fall of 1957. The thick, warm tapestry of aromas begins to blanket the inside of this little house located in Downey, California—robust odors of coffee, bacon, eggs, toast, biscuits, perhaps of pancakes or waffles, fresh and hot from the waffle machine, scents indigenous to dozens of such Saturday mornings behind him, and although the boy doesn't know it yet, too few of them yet to come. Because he is in the extra bedroom closest to the kitchen, the potent bouquet reaches him first. The kitchen is a fairly small enclave for the task at hand, but it is more than sufficient, because Grandpa enlarges it with his presence and art, turning it into a holy place where he performs his greatest work of grace amid withdrawing shadows chased by the light of a new day. Here beats the heart of the house, the "holy of holies," cluttered with religious artifacts; egg beaters, pots and pans, rolling pins, etc.—all the tools necessary for this elderly priest's sacrifice of thanksgiving and praise. Still, there is never much of a clatter of these things. Drawers are seldom banged, shelves are opened and closed gently. Being a notoriously early riser, Grandpa works with a reverential quietude born of respect for those who still slumber, and a deep sense of the morning's stillness and its call to calm venerable labor. The bedroom door is closed, but the boy can hear an occasional light thump, scrape, or bump, hear the groan of the furnace as it comes to life, and catch the faint familiar strains of "The Old Rugged Cross" which his grandpa never tires of whistling, nor the boy of hearing, because its haunting melody has always been a great comfort to him. From time to time the child hears the patter of slippered feet upon the creaking hardwood floor as the old man shuffles down the hallway past the boy's room and later, back again towards the kitchen.

The heat from the old floor-furnace eventually conquers the morning chill and it is just about then that the feast's incandescent incense reaches the farthest corners of the little house, stirring even the most sleepy-headed of its occupants. In the meantime, the boy rises from the warm cocoon of his bed, and drawn on as if still in a dream, filled with the warmth of familiarity and eager anticipation, he is barely aware that he has taken the time to brush the sleep from his eyes or put his slippers on. "T-bone, get up. Breakfast is almost ready." (T-bone is the boy's nickname.) This tender command is whispered just outside the boy's bedroom door, but there is no necessity for it except as a means of deepening the spell already being cast. It never fails to make the boy's heart beat faster when he hears the familiar voice calling him to the kitchen temple.

Of course Gramps knows the boy is up and the boy knows he knows, but the two of them can't help but attend to the rules of this whimsical rite. The boy smiles and senses that just outside the door his grandpa is doing the same. As part of this same sacramental performance, the boy does not leave his room immediately. He waits several beats...Now. It is time. The child quietly opens the door of his room, emerges into the hallway, and slowly makes his way towards the source of intoxicating scents that first woke him. Another familiar, very distinctive sound reaches him from the kitchen now...it is the dull, metallic zip of a tin key as it travels hesitantly around the lid of a can. Grandpa is adding Spam to the scrambled eggs. The boy moves past the living room and peers briefly in, seeing the fire dancing in the fireplace and the old upright piano against beige walls that are decorated with dozens of family photos. He imagines his mother and his Uncle Lanny sitting there at the piano playing "Heart and Soul," while the others—Heidi, Grandma, Daddy, Randy, Old Grandma, all of them—are there together laughing and clapping along. At last the boy enters the kitchen, and Grandpa, sensing the displacement of air behind him, turns from the cutting board and

A SLIGHT BREEZE CAME UP AND
DELIVERED THAT FAMILIAR SCENT TO MY
OLFACTORIES. SUDDENLY THERE WAS A
LUMP IN MY THROAT AND I WAS BROUGHT
UP SHORT, UNEXPECTEDLY OVERWHELMED
WITH AN EXQUISITELY SAD FEELING OF
MELANCHOLY AND A YEARNING FOR
SOMETHING UNNAMEABLE.

embraces the child. Then, as if by magic, a small portion of biscuit dough is produced. Grandfather, like a priest to his parishioner, ceremoniously places it into the boy's outstretched hand. They both smile. Then, as if on command, they pop the unbaked morsels into their mouths. Grandfather and grandson chew this bread of life slowly, and it is as if they are tasting it for the first time.

Vin Scully will be on the old RCA radio later in the day, and the boy and his grandpa will go to the garage to listen to the ballgame. Gramps will labor at his workbench as he whistles "Old Rugged Cross" and the boy will whistle it too (in his own fashion), pretending to be Grandpa busy at his workbench. In the meantime, the other family members are beginning to arrive and take their place at the breakfast table. They are all here together now, and no one is smiling more broadly than the man wearing Old Spice, the man with the apron on and the beautifully aged, callused hands painted with flour.

IV.

The first time I told my little girl the story of her great-grandpa and the little kitchen in Downey, we were together in the living room occupying the large stuffed chair in front of the bookshelf. She lay quietly in my lap with her head resting against my arm, barely stirring as I reminisced. Only after I had fallen silent did she look up at me with a wistful smile and brush tiny delicate tears from her eyes. Like her father, she is easily moved by sentiment.

"Daddy, why do we have to die?"

Uh oh. I have to handle this delicately. Quick, think of something. An image begins to form. "Sweetie, do you know what I think the first day of heaven will be like?" I ask her.

She sniffs and says, "What will it be like, Daddy?"

"Well, honey, to get into heaven the first thing we've got to do is—well...how should I put this..."

"Die, Daddy?" She speaks with the characteristic bluntness common to children, and she's much smarter than I tend to give her credit for.

"Well, sweetheart, yes," I say, starting to feel a little uncomfortable. I plunge on. "Anyway, it's more like falling asleep really, but different." She is silent, so I continue. "I believe that a lot of us grownups will be children again when we wake up in heaven." This connects with her big time.

"Really?" She smiles and leans in closer. "Will you be a kid again in heaven, Daddy?"

"I think so, honey, and God will wake us all up in a way that won't frighten us." I've got it now, but I'll have to struggle with a lump in my throat.

"How will He wake you up, Daddy?" Her voice is near a whisper.

"I know...at least I think I know how He'll do it." I'm looking deeply now into the innocent blue eyes of my beautiful daughter, but I'm seeing past them as well. "He'll wake me up with the smell of bacon and eggs and biscuits," I tell her, "and with a voice from the kitchen calling, 'T-bone, get up, breakfast is ready.'"

"Ahh," my little girl sighs, nestling deeper into my arms, and her sigh is so sweet...so full of love and of yearning, that I detect the faint scent of Old Spice and can hear once again the whisper of God.

KIM THOMAS

Kim's renderings on canvas capture the spirit of City on a Hill. *I'm glad she was commissioned for the task. Her art is intense, yet whimsical...serious, yet playful... exquisitely detailed, yet somehow simple. And I suspect these adjectives are descriptive of her personally as well.* ❧ *Yes, and this also: Kim fronts a band called Say So and authors books. She doesn't mind getting dirty now and then, either.*

Dirt

Why didn't God choose to form us out of gold, or marble dust, or precious diamonds? Why did He choose common dirt from which to form his image bearers?

Dirt is comprised of many elements, including dead and decaying things. In its own way dirt speaks of history. It records a story. It receives the seed, whose proximity to water either strains or feeds it. Dirt is moldable. It produces life, fruit, and vegetation. It is the medium of choice for growth for the God of creation. We were formed from it by His hand, and at the end of this life we will return to it. It is the connective tissue of humanity, and the path we walk upon.

There is so much of it. And such a variety. I've seen the red clay of Georgia and the white cliffs of Dover. I've walked the white beaches of the Gulf of Mexico and helicoptered over the black beaches of Hawaii. I've hiked the volcanic ash of the sleeping Mount Fuji and breathed the dust of west Texas. I've plunged my fleshy fingers into the compost-rich soil of my perennial garden. I suppose I could wear gloves — and my husband would prefer I did because I seem to get rashes from everything in my garden — but the connection of hand to earth is so transcendent that I don't dare prophylactically separate myself.

You may find my words melodramatic. "After all," you say, "it's only dirt." But I beg you to bear with me. I'm an artist by trade, and I have a note from my doctor saying it's okay to "feel" a little more than the average healthy person. Honestly, he said that. And then he prescribed an antidepressant for my serotonin-deprived clay vessel.

While God always intended that soil would bring forth life, we were never intended to have to toil in its production. What theologians refer to as the "fall of humankind" changed all that. It was mother Eve's choice to disobey that initiated this toiling, and my choices everyday continue to tag me as her daughter.

And I mourn this.

And so the soil of my heart must be worked if it is to once again bring forth life. But as the subtitle of Cornelius Plantinga's book on sin reminds us, this is "Not the Way It's Supposed to Be." Therefore I weep, as Jesus wept at the death of Lazarus, because death was never supposed to happen.

I mourn over the reality that when given the choice to do right or wrong, people do not always make the right choice. When I watch the news, I mourn the rampant sickness of violence. I cannot watch "Feed the Children" shows because they make me so unbearably sad. I am stunned that truth is no longer of great importance to so many people. I lament over the fact that people do not always do even the little things they say they will: return phone calls, pay their taxes, vote, eat their vegetables, or take care of themselves. And I ache that my own aptitude for wretchedness has caused me to speak hurtful words to my husband and soul mate. Words that, because of respect, I would never think of hurling at any other human being.

Sometimes this feeling of mourning sneaks up on me, making me tired and sad. The ugliness piles up so high that coping with everyday life becomes an act

of sheer will. I cannot even deal with my own ugliness, much less the fact that an entire population in Uganda is being slaughtered systematically. Sometimes, when I can't find the shirt I'm looking for in my closet, I end up collapsed in a heap, eyes streaming with tears, surprised that I am crying over such a trivial thing as a shirt. But I am not crying over a shirt.

I am crying, my husband says, because I long for heaven, where things are the way they are supposed to be. Heaven, the place of God's presence and our completeness, the place where justice and rightness are the rule. Where the children are all fed, bodies are mended, minds are whole, and our vision of truth and holiness is clear.

In case you think I'm sounding a little too obsessed with "poor me," let me set the record straight. While there are times I feel like a victim (after all, I am so oversensitive that I cry at the sight of roadkill), I also recognize that I am a participant in the crimes and immorality, the subjective and objective sins that have brought us all to this point. But there are times when it all hurts so much that I can't seem to get out of bed. And if I, a person who can't scrounge up any Anne Lamott-level traumas in my past, feel this way, then how must the people feel who have suffered so much more than me? How is it that they have continued to get out of bed?

Heaven is not unaware of the situation down here on planet earth. The Heavenly Three have not been sitting around in the eternal now waiting for me to point out that things are not as they should be. It was this awareness that caused God the Son, for the "joy set before him," to step out of heaven and into flesh and sacrifice Himself on a cross to set things right.

And it is because of this that I must learn to live "Thy kingdom come, Thy will be done, on earth as it is in heaven..." Heaven will be lovely, but for now I must live in my skin here on earth. And I must toil with the eroded and depleted soil of my heart so that it brings forth life.

HEAVEN IS NOT UNAWARE OF THE SITUATION DOWN HERE

ON PLANET EARTH. THE HEAVENLY THREE HAVE NOT BEEN

SITTING AROUND IN THE ETERNAL NOW WAITING FOR ME

TO POINT OUT THAT THINGS ARE NOT AS THEY SHOULD BE.

IT WAS THIS AWARENESS THAT CAUSED GOD THE SON, FOR

THE "JOY SET BEFORE HIM," TO STEP OUT OF HEAVEN

AND INTO FLESH AND SACRIFICE HIMSELF ON A CROSS

TO SET THINGS RIGHT.

Augustine has said we are restless until we find our rest in God. I must not look for rest anywhere else. Pascal wrote that there is a God-shaped vacuum within each of us. I must not attempt to fill my emptiness with cheap forgeries. And the apostle Paul instructed the Philippians this way: "Whatsoever things are true, honest, right, pure, lovely, of good repute, let your mind dwell on these things." I need to work these things into the soil of my life. To develop intentional habits of holiness. Everything else will ultimately disappoint me. Everything else will be found wanting, and pale. And I will be left longing and unsatisfied, in a heap in my closet.

When I was six years old, the Holy Spirit and four choruses of "Just As I Am" wooed me to walk down the carpeted aisle and publicly place my heart in the Savior's hands. And at the time, in my innocence, things seemed to be the way they were supposed to be. But over the next 35 years, subtle and not so subtle reminders have shown me more clearly why I need the Savior, not just for my eternal life, but in pursuing the daily fidelities of this life, because things are truly not as they are supposed to be.

The first Garden had rich and productive dirt. And God used that dirt to make us. But because of sin, it became fallow. So God the Son rescued us and brought us back to life. Because of this, my longings and mourning are not wrong, for they can lead me to recognize redemption in the path ahead.

The dirt path, the path that will lead me home.

DEREK WEBB
OF CAEDMON'S CALL

I appreciate the "specific" quality of Derek's lyrics (e.g., "Danny and I spent another late night over pancakes..." from his song, "Table For Two"). They make for original-ity...and Derek is a true original. But more importantly, he's someone who can be trusted. ❧ *Perceptive, talented and honest, Derek is about as unpretentious as anyone I've met—in a band, that is. "Hmmm, I wonder which white T-shirt he'll wear to the photo shoot?" Is he cynical? Well, more than slightly, but not in a way that feels mean-spirited. He has the ability to get me laughing pret-ty hard. In fact, my experience in the studio with Caedmon's Call was entirely enjoyable.*

Resting in the Providence

I remember that when I was a child I thought I was a good person. I had grown up like most kids do, stumbling through adolescence and a brief but intense period of rebellion, with the occasional good deed to keep a spark of hope alive in the eyes of my parents. My experience with the church had been intriguing, but inconsequential. I possessed a work-ing knowledge of Christian lingo, but no real faith — nothing that could be considered even the lowest grade of fire insurance. I frequently ran in Christian circles and even considered myself one, I think. Whatever they were, I was. However, my Christianity was like a T-shirt that I could put on and take off depending on my surroundings. After being confirmed into the Methodist church I didn't think it necessary to give much thought to spiritual things. I had been there and done that. I'd reached a great level of comfort with spiritual matters, and an even greater level of self-deception.

Sometime near the end of my sophomore year of high school, some friends and I were driving on a dark Texas highway en route to Waco. We played together in a band and shared much in common. One thing we did not have in common was our ages. These guys were much older than I was and had been drinking. The lead singer and I were traveling in a truck out in front while the others followed in a second car. Suddenly we came upon some cattle standing right in the middle of the road. We had no time to react and collided with them. We were moving just fast enough to total both the truck and the poor cows we met so unexpectedly. The driver, in maternal fashion, grabbed my arm to keep me from flying through the windshield, as I was not wearing a seat belt. Although he probably saved my life, my friend could not restrain my head from shattering the windshield. The gash on my head bled profusely as they pulled me from the wreck. The guys were able to get me on my knees on the side of the road and flag down a passing car for help.

In the aftermath of the accident a man stopped to pray with me, which I faintly remember, asking God to spare my life and save my soul. As much as I appreciated this man's gesture, I do remember thinking that I was not a boy in need of salvation. He was wasting his time on me.

As a result of this episode, the band that I was in broke up, freeing me up for the summer. Under the influence of my older brother, my parents sent me kicking and screaming to a Young Life Camp in Colorado for a week. The biggest problem that I faced there was the fact that I began to understand what the speaker was really talking about and found myself compelled to believe it. I was very familiar with his topic, but unfamiliar with his angle. This was the first time I remembered hearing of the possibility of a personal relationship with my Creator by way of Jesus Christ. I found myself wooed by the idea that

I was worth so much to God that He would take on flesh and come to earth to save me. Later that night, in the quiet solitude of my cabin there in the mountains, I asked for Christ's intercession on my behalf. At that moment I felt a peace with which I was totally unfamiliar. I felt that my life was finally under control and that I was safe. As we all know, those moments don't tend to last very long.

Fast forward seven years or so. Few people ever get to meet their heroes. I've had the privilege of meeting a few of mine. One of them was a man by the name of Rich Mullins. He was a poet/philosopher with an incredible gift. He could write words that seemed to come right from God's mouth to my ears. My band, Caedmon's Call, had the great pleasure of crossing paths with Rich not long after recording one of his songs, "Hope to Carry On," for our first record. Our record label had decided to put together a video for the song and we immediately thought that would provide a great excuse to spend some quality time with our long-time hero. Because of the time we were able to spend together on the video shoot, and as a result of a surrealistic set that I played at the

Cornerstone Festival in 1997 (where Rich Mullins and Mitch McVicker joined me onstage for a memorable rendition of "Hope to Carry On,") Rich and I developed a strange and fast friendship. We would even hear from him on occasion when he was playing concerts near our hometown of Houston. Then, on September 19, 1997 I received some shocking news. Rich Mullins, my hero, my friend, had been killed driving on a highway just outside of Peoria, Illinois. It was beyond belief. I remember being in a shopping mall in Houston when I heard the news from my brother and collapsing against a wall for 15 or 20 minutes out of shock. But the implications of this tragedy stretched much farther than just my emotions; it shook my theology of the providence of God to its foundations. Where was God on that dark Illinois highway? Was He in control of this "random" accident? If so, why did He allow it? If not, who was in control? Needless to say, I spent many sleepless nights mulling over these important questions and praying that God would reveal His truth to me. Many were saying that "it wasn't Rich's time," and that "he had more songs to write," and, "more to say," and I found myself reluctantly agreeing.

But as easy as it was to think that Rich had more to accomplish in his life and that a random accident robbed him of the chance, it just wasn't consistent with what I knew to be true of God, of His character, and of the way He governs His creation. The thing that I struggled with the most was my own emotion in regard to the incident. Now don't get me wrong; I don't mean that the way we feel about things that hurt us doesn't matter to God. By no means. God cares deeply about the way we feel. My point is that the way we feel about something doesn't make it true or false. For example, my belief that Jesus Christ is the Son of God doesn't make it true or valid; it's true simply because it is. My belief in it is incidental to its being true; my belief adds nothing. The same can be said of gravity. I can feel that gravity is unfair, somehow infringing on my liberty as a human being, restricting me to walking upon the earth and denying me the ability to float into the air or fly. However, if I walk off the edge of a cliff we both know what will happen. My disbelief in gravity will not help me in the slightest at that moment, and I will plunge to my death. Do my feelings regarding gravity or my emotion towards it have any bearing on it being true or not? Decidedly not.

It is much the same with the things of God. Job 14:5 says that man's "days are determined, the number of his months is with You; You have appointed his limits, so that he cannot pass" (NKJV), and in Matthew 10:28-31 we're told that we should "not fear those who kill the body but cannot kill the soul. But rather fear Him who is able to destroy both soul and body in hell. Are not two sparrows sold for a copper coin? And not one of them falls to the ground apart from your Father's will. But the very hairs of your head are all numbered. Do not fear therefore; you are of more value than many sparrows" (NKJV). As this passage assures us, God is completely in control of the seemingly random events that we witness around us. He is the same God whom Isaiah speaks of as "declaring the end from the beginning, and from ancient times things that are not yet done, saying, 'My counsel shall stand, and I will do all My pleasure'" (Isaiah 46:10 NKJV). Here was the truth that I was seeking, the truth that my emotions were blinding me from seeing. Rich Mullins did not have one more thing to say or even one more song to write. He fulfilled God's purposes for his life to the very letter. The night that Rich was killed, God was not frantically scrambling around heaven saying, "Oh my! Someone killed Rich

GOD'S WAYS ARE OFTEN MYSTERIOUS TO US.

WE ARE HIS FINITE CREATURES, SO WE MUST PRAY DAILY

FOR THE GRACE TO SEE THE UNDERLYING PROVIDENCE

OF OUR FATHER IN EVEN THE DARKEST AND

CLOUDIEST OF TIMES.

Mullins! Who will bring the gospel to all the people that I had planned for Rich to touch with his music? I have to hurry or all will be lost!" On the contrary, God was there on the highway that night with Rich, perfectly orchestrating the events that would grant Rich's most enduring prayer, to be home with his sweet Father.

At this point in my life I can look back on the accident I had on that Texas highway without anger and confusion but with praise, knowing that God was perfectly orchestrating the events that would lead to my salvation. In the same way I can now see God's hand in ushering Rich Mullins into heaven. God's ways are often mysterious to us. We are His finite creatures, so we must pray daily for the grace to see the underlying providence of our Father in even the darkest and cloudiest of times.

"Let everything that has breath praise the LORD."
(Psalm 150:6 NIV)

Dear Friends,

I first got to know Don Rogers at Azusa Pacific University in the late '70s, as we were classmates, both involved in school music groups. Don was a trombone player and a ventriloquist! I immediately appreciated his sweet spirit and eventually grew to admire him as a devoted servant of Christ.

In 1990, my wife and I attended a church where Don was serving as interim pastor. We were profoundly touched by his ministry. Don is an inspiring leader and communicator. I remember some of his messages even to this day!

So when Don made plans to embark on a new ministry in East Africa, we were eager to lend our limited support. It's been exciting to follow the growth and success of Empowering Lives International over the past several years. Many times I've been brought to tears just reading the newsletters describing their challenging work in two small, impoverished villages in Kenya. Don, his wife, Amy, and several co-workers are putting God's love into action! Through evangelism, discipleship, and community development projects, they continue to make tremendous progress in their efforts to alleviate hunger, disease, and spiritual darkness. Empowering Lives International is bringing hope and help to people in desperate need. Truly!

I'm so pleased that the royalties from this book will be offered in support of this amazing ministry! And it's my privilege to encourage you to participate as well. Please be sure to check out their website!

Steve Hindalong

EMPOWERING LIVES INTERNATIONAL (ELI)

IS A NON-DENOMINATIONAL, NON-PROFIT, CHRISTIAN ORGANIZATION MINISTERING AMONG THE POOR IN EAST AFRICA. ELI STAFF AND SHORT TERM VOLUNTEERS SERVE TOGETHER WITH PEOPLE IN THE EAST AFRICAN VILLAGES, SEEKING TO BRING AN EFFECTIVE, CULTURALLY APPROPRIATE SOLUTION TO THE CHALLENGES OF POVERTY AND SPIRITUAL DARKNESS.

Endeavoring to actively express God's love, ELI integrates evangelistic efforts, discipleship, and community projects designed to provide the encouragement, skills, and ideas necessary for the African people to achieve and maintain a self-sufficient status. Training centers stationed throughout the Kenya and Tanzania areas offer courses from farming, irrigation, and animal care to church leadership and youth ministry development.

Royalties from the sale of this book have been generously donated by the author and contributors of *City on a Hill* to the ministry of Empowering Lives International. Through the purchase of this book, you are financially partnering with the life-changing difference ELI is making in the world. For further information on how you can positively impact developing countries through prayer, financial support, or personal involvement through short-term service contact:

Empowering Lives International
PO Box A
Garden Grove, CA 92842
(909)390-5121

www.empoweringlives.org